Discrimination

An OPPOSING VIEWPOINTS® Guide

Lauri S. Friedman, *Book Editor*

OPPOSING
VIEWPOINTS®
SERIES

GREENHAVEN PRESS
A part of Gale, Cengage Learning

GALE
CENGAGE Learning

Detroit • New York • San Francisco • New Haven, Conn • Waterville, Maine • London

Christine Nasso, *Publisher*
Elizabeth Des Chenes, *Managing Editor*

© 2009 Greenhaven Press, a part of Gale, Cengage Learning

Gale and Greenhaven Press are registered trademarks used herein under license.

For more information, contact:
Greenhaven Press
27500 Drake Rd.
Farmington Hills, MI 48331-3535
Or you can visit our Internet site at gale.cengage.com

For product information and technology assistance, contact us at

Gale Customer Support, 1-800-877-4253
For permission to use material from this text or product, submit all requests online at www.cengage.com/permissions

Further permissions questions can be emailed to permissionrequest@cengage.com

Articles in Greenhaven Press anthologies are often edited for length to meet page requirements. In addition, original titles of these works are changed to clearly present the main thesis and to explicitly indicate the author's opinion. Every effort is made to ensure that Greenhaven Press accurately reflects the original intent of the authors. Every effort has been made to trace the owners of copyrighted material.

Cover image Douglas McFadd/Getty Images.

LIBRARY OF CONGRESS CATALOGING-IN-PUBLICATION DATA

Discrimination / Lauri S. Friedman, book editor.
    p. cm. — (Writing the critical essay: an opposing viewpoints guide)
  Includes bibliographical references and index.
  ISBN 978-0-7377-4403-3 (hardcover)
  1. Discrimination—United States—Junvenile literature. I. Friedman, Lauri S.
  HN90.S6.D573 2009
  305—dc22
                                                                   2008048356

Printed in the United States of America
1 2 3 4 5 6 7 13 12 10 11 10 09

CONTENTS

Section Two: Model Essays and Writing Exercises

Section Three: Supporting Research Material

Examining the state of writing and how it is taught in the United States was the official purpose of the National Commission on Writing in America's Schools and Colleges. The commission, made up of teachers, school administrators, business leaders, and college and university presidents, released its first report in 2003. "Despite the best efforts of many educators," commissioners argued, "writing has not received the full attention it deserves." Among the findings of the commission was that most fourth-grade students spent less than three hours a week writing, that three-quarters of high school seniors never receive a writing assignment in their history or social studies classes, and that more than 50 percent of first-year students in college have problems writing error-free papers. The commission called for a "cultural sea change" that would increase the emphasis on writing for both elementary and secondary schools. These conclusions have made some educators realize that writing must be emphasized in the curriculum. As colleges are demanding an ever-higher level of writing proficiency from incoming students, schools must respond by making students more competent writers. In response to these concerns, the SAT, an influential standardized test used for college admissions, required an essay for the first time in 2005.

Books in the Writing the Critical Essay: An Opposing Viewpoints Guide series use the patented Opposing Viewpoints format to help students learn to organize ideas and arguments and to write essays using common critical writing techniques. Each book in the series focuses on a particular type of essay writing—including expository, persuasive, descriptive, and narrative—that students learn while being taught both the five-paragraph essay as well as longer pieces of writing that have an opinionated focus. These guides include everything necessary to help students research, outline, draft, edit, and ultimately write successful essays across the curriculum, including essays for the SAT.

Using Opposing Viewpoints

This series is inspired by and builds upon Greenhaven Press's acclaimed Opposing Viewpoints series. As in the parent series, each book in the Writing the Critical Essay series focuses on a timely and controversial social issue that provides lots of opportunities for creating thought-provoking essays. The first section of each volume begins with a brief introductory essay that provides context for the opposing viewpoints that follow. These articles are chosen for their accessibility and clearly stated views. The thesis of each article is made explicit in the article's title and is accentuated by its pairing with an opposing or alternative view. These essays are both models of persuasive writing techniques and valuable research material that students can mine to write their own informed essays. Guided reading and discussion questions help lead students to key ideas and writing techniques presented in the selections.

The second section of each book begins with a preface discussing the format of the essays and examining characteristics of the featured essay type. Model five-paragraph and longer essays then demonstrate that essay type. The essays are annotated so that key writing elements and techniques are pointed out to the student. Sequential, step-by-step exercises help students construct and refine thesis statements; organize material into outlines; analyze and try out writing techniques; write transitions, introductions, and conclusions; and incorporate quotations and other researched material. Ultimately, students construct their own compositions using the designated essay type.

The third section of each volume provides additional research material and writing prompts to help the student. Additional facts about the topic of the book serve as a convenient source of supporting material for essays. Other features help students go beyond the book for their research. Like other Greenhaven Press books, each book in the Writing the Critical Essay series includes bibliographic listings of relevant periodical articles, books, Web sites, and organizations to contact.

Writing the Critical Essay: An Opposing Viewpoints Guide will help students master essay techniques that can be used in any discipline.

The New Face of Civil Rights and Discrimination

Discrimination is practiced against innumerable types of people and comes in many forms. Though it is often associated with racial and ethnic prejudice, discrimination often goes far beyond this common form of the practice. People can be discriminated against because of their age—employers have been sued because of their reluctance to hire people who are older, believing they are out of touch with industry innovations. People can also be discriminated against, both in the workplace and in society, if they have a disability. Gender, religion, and national origin are other qualifiers that have provoked unjust discrimination throughout the ages. While sexual orientation has long been a cause of discrimination, emerging debates over same-sex marriage—whether two people of the same sex should be allowed to legally marry one another—have taken center stage in national discussions about discrimination and civil rights. In fact, many claim that same-sex marriage is the new face of the civil rights struggle.

Same-sex marriage was first legalized by the state of Massachusetts in 2004 and next by California in 2008. (though gay marriage in that state is on hold due to a proposition that passed in the November elections defining marriage as between a man and a woman). The California State Supreme Court legalized gay marriage because it found that a state law that defined marriage as a union between a man and a woman was an unconstitutional form of gender discrimination. Similarly, when the Massachusetts State Supreme Judicial Court voted to legalize gay marriage in that state, the court did so because it said it would be unconstitutional to "deny the protections, benefits and obligations conferred by civil marriage to two individuals of the same sex."[1] In other words, in the eyes of these two courts, to deny gay couples the rights that come with marriage constitutes discrimination and the creation of a second-class citizenry, both of which the states' constitutions prohibit.

Advocates for same-sex marriage agree that denying gay couples the right to marry infringes on their civil rights to life, liberty, and the pursuit of happiness and in this sense is discriminatory. For these reasons, the struggle to legalize same-sex marriage is often compared to the black civil rights movement of the 1960s, when blacks, through important acts of civil disobedience, overcame institutionalized discrimination that denied them basic rights and relegated them to second-class citizenship. Those who support the legalization of same-sex marriage see many parallels between the black Americans of the 1960s and the gay Americans of the twenty-first century, calling both groups victims of institutionalized discrimination that denies them equality and justice. Such is the perspective of Victoria A. Brownworth, a lesbian journalist who has written extensively on the matter. "Every heterosexual citizen is granted rights I am not privy to simply by virtue of her or his sexual orientation," complains Brownworth. "That is wrong. That is unjust. That is a violation of my civil rights as an American citizen and the rights of my friends as American citizens. We should all have the option of marrying the person we love."[2]

But is it discriminatory to prevent same-sex couples from marrying? Not according to people such as columnist Jeff Jacoby, who argue that same-sex marriage is not a civil rights issue at all. Jacoby and others reject claims that the struggle for gay marriage has anything in common with the black civil rights movement of the 1960s. In that era, blacks sought to achieve the same exact rights and services that white Americans had. But gay Americans are not technically excluded from the tradition of marriage, it is argued; they may marry a person of the opposite sex any time they choose. What gay Americans want to do is change the definition to include themselves, which Jacoby says makes the matter decid-

edly not a civil rights issue: "They don't want to accept or reject marriage on the same terms that it is available to everyone else," says Jacoby. "They want it on entirely new terms. They want it to be given a meaning it has never before had. . . . Whatever else that may be, it isn't civil rights."[3] Therefore, gay marriage opponents conclude that excluding same-sex unions from the tradition of marriage is not a violation of civil rights or justice; it is simply the natural limits of the institution as they have always existed.

Whether denying homosexuals the right to marry constitutes discrimination is sure to be a hot issue in the coming years, as every election season has increasing numbers of voters weighing in on the issue. Between ballot initiatives that propose to legalize same-sex marriage or define marriage as an institution between a man and a woman, the controversy over whether denying

Three of the seven gay couples who sued the state of Massachusetts react at a press conference to the state's Supreme Judicial Court ruling that same-sex couples are legally entitled to wed.

Critics of same-sex marriage say that the issue is not about civil rights but that homosexuals want to give new meaning to traditional marriage.

homosexuals the right to marry is discriminatory has etched itself into the national conversation. Same-sex marriage is just one example of how discrimination issues stretch far beyond issues of race and ethnicity. It is also just one of the issues explored in *Writing the*

Critical Essay: Discrimination. Readers will examine other forms of discrimination, such as racial, ethnic, religious, and gender discrimination, and form their own opinions on the matter. Model essays and thought-provoking writing exercises help readers write their own narrative essays on this important subject.

Notes

1. *Hillary Goodridge et al. v. Massachusetts Department of Public Health*, 440 Mass. 309, 798 NE2d 941 (2003). www.law.umkc.edu/faculty/projects/ftrials/conlaw/ Goodridge.html.

2. Victoria A. Brownworth, "Civil Disobedience = Civil Rights," *Curve*, June 2004.

3. Jeff Jacoby, "Gay Marriage Isn't Civil Rights," *Boston Globe*, March 7, 2004.

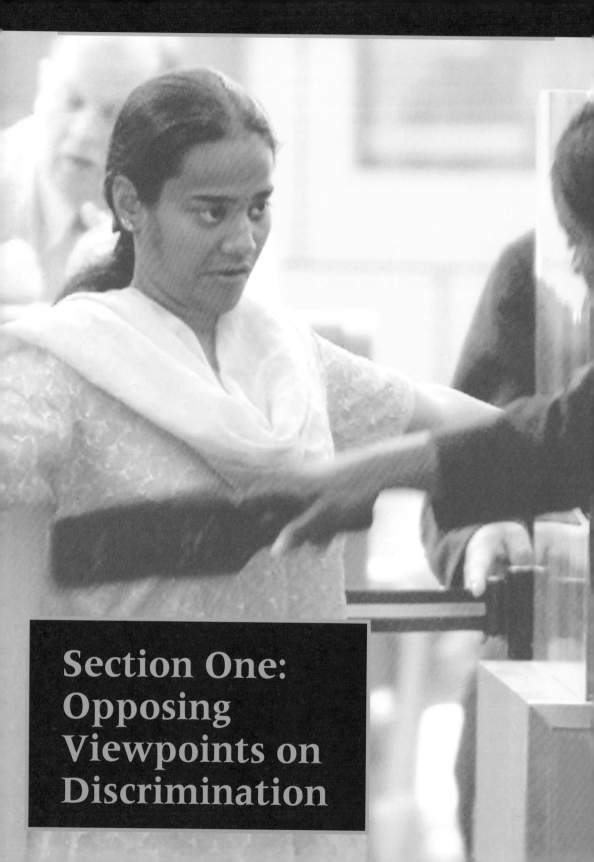

Section One:
Opposing
Viewpoints on
Discrimination

Discrimination Is a Serious Problem for the Black Community

Earl Ofari Hutchinson

In the following essay Earl Ofari Hutchinson argues that discrimination is a serious problem for black males. He discusses how young black males have the highest unemployment rate of any group in the United States, nearly double that of their white counterparts. Hutchinson says these high unemployment rates are a result of widespread, systematic discrimination of employers against black job candidates. He cites several studies that found employers hold consistently negative attitudes about black job candidates and avoid hiring them no matter their qualifications. Hutchinson concludes that illegal immigration has not stolen jobs from young black Americans—rather, they have been the victims of American employers' discrimination and bigotry.

Hutchinson is a journalist, author, and broadcaster. He has written nine books about the African American experience and currently serves as the president of the National Alliance for Positive Action, a multi-ethnic public issues advocacy group.

Consider the following questions:

1. What percent of young black males are unemployed, as reported by the author?
2. According to Hutchinson, who is more likely to be hired for a job: a white man with a criminal record or a black man without one?
3. Name at least five adjectives the author says employers use to describe black employees.

Earl Ofari Hutchinson, "Discrimination, Not Illegal Immigration, Fuels Black Job Crisis," *New America Media*, April 24, 2006. Copyright © Pacific News Service. Reproduced by permission.

The battle continues to rage between economists, politicians, immigrant rights activists and black anti-immigration activists over whether illegal immigrants are the major cause of double-digit joblessness among poor, unskilled, young black males. The battle lines are so tight and impassioned that black anti-immigration activists plan a march for jobs for American-born blacks on April 28 [2006] in Los Angeles. This is a direct counter to the planned mass action three days later by some immigrant rights groups.

According to Labor Department reports, nearly 40 percent of young black males are unemployed. Despite the Bush administration's boast that its tax cut and economic policies have resulted in the creation of more than 100,000 new jobs, black unemployment still remains the highest of any group in America. Black male unemployment for the past decade has been nearly double that of white males. The picture is grimmer for young black males.

Unemployed African Americans apply for jobs. According to the U.S. Department of Labor, 40 percent of young black males are unemployed.

Discrimination in the Workplace

Black unemployment rates are consistently higher than white unemployment rates and the national average.

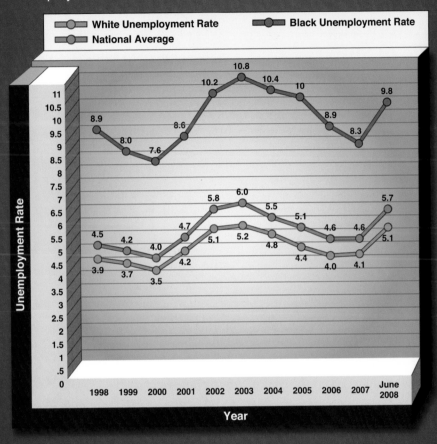

Taken from: U.S. Department of Labor, Bureau of Labor Statistics, July 2008.

Racial Discrimination in the Workplace

But several years before the immigration combatants squared off, then University of Wisconsin graduate researcher Devah Pager pointed the finger in another direction, a direction that makes most employers squirm. And that's toward the persistent and deep racial discrimination in the workplace. Pager found that black men without a criminal record are less likely to find a job than white men with criminal records.

Pager's finger-point at discrimination as the main reason for the racial disparity in hiring set off howls of protest from employers, trade groups and even a Nobel Prize winner. They lambasted her for faulty research. Her sample was much too small, they said, and the questions too vague. They pointed to the ocean of state and federal laws that ban racial discrimination. But in 2005 Pager, now a sociologist at Princeton duplicated her study. She surveyed nearly 1,500 private employers in New York City.

She used teams of black and white testers, standardized resumes, and she followed up their visits with telephone interviews with employers. These are the standard methods researchers use to test racial discrimination. The results were exactly the same as in her earlier study, despite the fact that New York has some of the nation's toughest laws against job discrimination.

> ## Black Americans Continue to Suffer Discrimination
>
> Among racial minorities, African Americans are the most segregated. Demographers, interpreting the 2000 census, say 65 percent of all black people would have to move in order to be evenly distributed among whites. Only the black poor experience "hyper-segregation"—extreme ghetto isolation, a parallel universe of violence and social distress.
>
> Sheryll D. Cashin, "Living Separately and Unequally," *Los Angeles Times*, July 6, 2004.

Employers Discriminate Against Black Workers

Dumping the blame for the chronic job crisis of young, poor black men on undocumented immigrants stokes the passions and hysteria of immigration reform opponents, but it also lets employers off the hook for discrimination. And it's easy to see how that could happen. The mountain of federal and state anti-discrimination laws, affirmative action programs and successful employment discrimination lawsuits give the public the impression that job discrimination is a relic of a shameful, racist past.

But that isn't the case, and Pager's study is hardly isolated proof of that. Countless research studies, the Urban League's annual State of Black America report, a 2005 Human Rights Watch report and the numerous discrimination complaints reviewed by the Equal Employment Opportunity Commission over the past decade reveal that employers have devised endless dodges to evade anti-discrimination laws. That includes rejecting applicants by their names or areas of the city they live in. Black applicants may be incorrectly told that jobs advertised were filled already.

In a seven-month comprehensive university study of the hiring practices of hundreds of Chicago area employers, a few years before Pager's graduate study, many top company officials when interviewed said they would not hire blacks. When asked to assess the work ethic of white, black and Latino employees by race, nearly 40 percent of the employer's ranked blacks dead last.

"Illiterate, Dishonest, and Unskilled"

The employers routinely described blacks as being "unskilled," "uneducated," "illiterate," "dishonest," "lacking initiative," "involved with gangs and drugs" or

National Urban League president Hugh B. Price talks during a news conference about "The State of Black America" report and its findings. While considerable progress has been made, major discrimination obstacles remain.

"unstable," of having "no family values" and being "poor role models." The consensus among these employers was that blacks brought their alleged pathologies to the work place, and were to be avoided at all costs. Not only white employers express such views; researchers found that black business owners shared many of the same negative attitudes.

Other surveys have found that a substantial number of non-white business owners also refuse to hire blacks. Their bias effectively closed out another area of employment to thousands of blacks, solely based on their color.

This only tells part of the sorry job picture for many poor blacks. The Congressional Black Caucus reports that at least half of all unemployed black workers have been out of work for a year or more. Many have given up looking for work. The Census does not count them among the unemployed.

The dreary job picture for the unskilled and marginally skilled urban poor, especially the black poor is compounded by the racially skewed attitudes of small and large employers. Even if there was not a single illegal immigrant in America, that attitude insures that many black job seekers would still find themselves shut out.

Analyze the essay:

1. Hutchinson relies on several studies to make his argument that workplace discrimination is a serious problem for black American males. Make a list of all the studies he cites and how he used their data. Which study offered the most convincing supporting evidence? Which offered the least?

2. In his discussion Hutchinson did not use any quotes, anecdotes, or real-life examples. If you were to rewrite this essay to include such details, what kinds of stories would you use, and where would you put them?

Discrimination Is Not the Black Community's Primary Problem

Viewpoint Two

Walter E. Williams

In the following essay, Walter E. Williams argues that although blacks have faced racism in the past, discrimination is not the main source of their problems today. According to Williams, in the twenty-first century African Americans are wealthy, successful, and hold positions of enormous power, as is evidenced by the 2008 election of President Barack Obama. Williams says the problems that plague the black community today—illegitimacy, single-parent households, high school-dropout rates, gangs, drugs, and crime—cannot be blamed on discrimination but are the result of "black victimhood," the notion that white people have imposed these problems on blacks. Williams does not see how discrimination can be blamed for the community's contemporary problems. For example, he points out that in the early 1990s—when discrimination against blacks was rampant—black families were much more stable and cohesive than they are today. Similarly, black schools receive the same amount of funding as white schools, so Williams is unwilling to blame a lack of resources for the problem of poor school performance. He calls on African Americans to stop blaming discrimination for their problems and to replace notions of victimhood with positive thinking and action. He also calls on white America to stop feeling unnecessarily guilty for problems in the black community.

Walter E. Williams is a nationally syndicated columnist and the author of the book *More Liberty Means Less Government*.

Consider the following questions:
1. If the African American community were a country, what ranking does Williams say it would have in terms of its wealth?
2. What percent of black children are raised in two-parent households, according to the author?
3. What percent of all homicides are committed by blacks, according to Williams? What percent of all homicides are directed toward blacks?

Despite the fact that President-elect Barack Obama's vision for our nation leaves a lot to be desired, the fact that he was elected represents a remarkable national achievement. When the War of 1861 ended, neither a former slave nor slave owner would have believed it possible for a black to be elected president in a mere century and a half, if ever. I'm sure that my grandparents, born in the 1880s, or my parents, born in the 1910s, would not have believed it possible for a black to be president and neither did I for most of my 72 years.

Blacks Have Come a Long Way
That's not the only progress. If one totaled black earnings, and consider blacks a separate nation, he would have found that in 2005 black Americans earned $644 billion, making them the world's 16th richest nation. That's just behind Australia but ahead of Netherlands, Belgium and Switzerland. Black Americans have been chief executives of some of the world's largest and richest cities such as New York, Chicago, Los Angeles, Philadelphia and Washington, D.C. Gen. Colin Powell, appointed Joint Chief of Staff in October 1989, headed the world's mightiest military and later became U.S. Secretary of State, and was succeeded by Condoleezza Rice, another black. A few black Americans are among the world's richest

people and many are some of the world's most famous personalities. These gains, over many difficult hurdles, speak well not only of the intestinal fortitude of a people but of a nation in which these gains were possible. They could not have been achieved anywhere else.

Discrimination Does Not Hold Blacks Down

Acknowledgement of these achievements is not to deny that a large segment of the black community faces enormous problems. But as I have argued, most of today's

Actor-comedian Bill Cosby believes the black community must let go of the notion of "black victimhood" and replace it with positive thinking and action.

The Black Community Should Take Responsibility for Itself

Racism is no longer the major problem facing American blacks. . . . What is? A list of likely culprits would surely include the collapse of the black family, the failure of the public schools and black-on-black crime.

Linda Chavez, "The NAACP Has Lost Its Vision," Townhall.com, July 13, 2003.

problems have little or nothing to do with racial discrimination. That's not to say that every vestige of racial discrimination has been eliminated but as my colleague Dr. John McWhorter said in "End of Racism?" *Forbes* (11/5/08), "There are also rust and mosquitoes, and there always will be. Life goes on." The fact that the nation elected a black president hopefully might turn our attention away from the false notion that discrimination explains the problems of a large segment of the black community to the real problems that have absolutely nothing to do with discrimination.

The illegitimacy rate among blacks stands at about 70 percent. Less than 40 percent of black children are raised

Discrimination Is Not the Black Community's Main Problem

A 2007 Pew Research/NPR poll found that the majority of whites, blacks, and Hispanics believe discrimination is not the reason blacks cannot get ahead.

Main reason many blacks cannot get ahead is. . . .	All adults	Whites	Blacks	Hispanics
Racial discrimination	19%	15%	30%	24%
Blacks responsible for their own condition	66%	71%	53%	59%
Neither/both	9%	8%	14%	8%
Don't know/ no answer	6%	6%	3%	9%

Taken from: Pew Research Center and National Public Radio, November 2007.

Successful black businesses provide jobs and strengthen the black community's well-being.

in two-parent households. Those are major problems but they have nothing to do with racial discrimination. During the early 1900s, illegitimacy was a tiny fraction of today's rate and black families were just as stable as white families. Fraudulent education is another problem, where the average black high school senior can read, write and compute no better than a white seventh-grader. It can hardly be blamed on discrimination. Black schools receive the same funding as white schools and most of the teachers and staffs are black and the schools are often in cities where the mayor and the city council are mostly black. Crime is a major problem. Blacks commit about 50 percent of all homicides and 95 percent of their victims are blacks.

Stop Feeling Guilty

Tragically, many black politicians and a civil rights industry have a vested interest in portraying the poor socio-economic outcomes for many blacks as problems rooted in racial discrimination. One of the reasons they are able to get away with such deception is because there are so many guilt-ridden white people. Led by guilt, college administrators, employers and others in leadership positions, in the name of diversity, buy into nonsense such as lowering standards, racial preferences and acceptance of behavior standards they wouldn't accept from whites. Maybe the election of a black president will help white people over their guilt feelings so they can stop acting like fools in their relationships with black people.

Analyze the essay:

1. At the end of the essay, Williams discusses the role guilt has played in establishing racial preferences, affirmative action policies, and other standards of acceptance for the black community. Sum up Williams's position on this matter. Then, state whether or not you agree with his point of view.

2. Williams rejects the notion that blacks have been victimized and urges them to take responsibility for rectifying the hardships the community has faced. How do you think Earl Ofari Hutchinson, the author of the previous essay, would respond to this suggestion?

Racially Profiling Arabs and Muslims Is Discriminatory

Hussein Ibish

In the following essay Hussein Ibish argues that racial profiling is a discriminatory practice that is wrongly used to target Muslim and Arab peoples. He says when police look for potential criminals based solely on their appearance, they fail to pick up on more telling clues, such as suspicious behavior. Ibish provides examples of terrorists who have been from all races, nations, and backgrounds, noting that racial profiling would not have been effective against these people. When police target one ethnicity over another, therefore, they reduce their ability to catch real criminals. Finally, Ibish says that more often than not, racial profiling leads police to arrest or even kill the wrong people—such as Brazilian Jean Charles de Menezes, who was mistakenly shot dead by British police because they assumed him to be a Pakistani terrorist. For all these reasons, Ibish concludes that racial profiling is not a good law enforcement technique and is morally wrong.

Hussein Ibish is the vice chair of the Progressive Muslim Union of North America, a liberal Muslim organization. He is also communications director for the American-Arab Anti-Discrimination Committee (ADC), the nation's largest Arab American membership organization.

Consider the following questions:

1. Why, in Ibish's opinion, is it impossible to say that Arabs or Muslims look alike?
2. What percent of American Muslims are African American, according to Ibish?
3. Who are Richard Reid, John Walker Lindh, and Jose Padilla, and how do they factor into the author's argument?

Hussein Ibish, "Let's not spite our face with profiling," *Daily Star* (Beirut, Lebanon), August 15, 2005. Reproduced by permission of the author.

If anyone ever wondered what demons lurking in American culture might have possessed the singer Michael Jackson to bleach his skin and destroy his once-noble African features through a series of bizarre plastic surgeries—to literally cut off his nose to spite his face—all they need to do is cast their attention on the debate that has ensued in recent weeks in the United States about "racial profiling."

An Old, Bad Practice Is Back

Racial profiling is a long-discredited American law-enforcement technique whereby police identify individuals as suspects based on their apparent race, ethnicity, age, and other simple identity criteria. This was a central feature of abuse against African-American and Latino populations throughout the country, but is now illegal and has few defenders. Except where Arabs and Muslims are concerned.

Following the [July 7, 2005] attacks on the London mass transport system, the New York City subway instituted random searches of passengers, as a reassurance to the public and a deterrent to terrorists. Many American commentators have condemned this policy, as well as the U.S. government's entire counterterrorism strategy, for not engaging in racial profiling against Arab and Muslim Americans.

Racial Profiling Is Easy for Terrorists to Beat

Behavior profiling is much more effective than racial profiling . . . because it's not unusual for terrorist groups to outsource their operations to individuals or groups who don't fit the expected racial or ethnic profile.

Kim Zetter, "Why Racial Profiling Doesn't Work," Salon.com, August 22, 2005. http://dir.salon.com/story/news/feature/2005/08/22/racial_profiling/.

There Is No Arab or Muslim "Look"

Many Americans are used to thinking in simplistic terms about race and ethnicity, of living in a world divided between black and white in which identity is obvious from pigmentation and can be discerned at a glance. Proponents of profiling have proven amazingly resistant to understanding that identifying

Arab and Muslim Americans based on appearance is simply impossible.

Leaving aside the fact that over half of the Arabs in the United States are Christians, Arabs can resemble almost any group of southern Europeans, Latin Americans, Central and South Asians, or Africans.

Even more preposterous would be any attempt to identify Muslims by appearance, since Muslims come from almost every part of the world, and constitute a fifth of humanity. And, since about a third of American Muslims are African-Americans, any futile attempt at profiling of Muslims, especially in urban areas such as New York City, would immediately degenerate into yet another way of profiling black people.

The New York City Muslim community meets with the FBI Counter-Terrorism Task Force to discuss their concerns about immigration policy, racial profiling, and harassment of American Muslims.

The Fallacy of "They All Look Alike" Logic

Washington Post columnist Charles Krauthammer wants racial profiling but would "immediately exempt Hispanics, Scandinavians and East Asians," as if Hispanics were readily distinguishable from Arabs and South Asians.

And, as his *Washington Post* colleague Colby King pointed out, "by eliminating Scandinavians from his list of obvious terror suspects, Krauthammer would have authorities give a pass to all white people."

Supporters of racial profiling cling to the idea that you can tell who is an Arab, and even a Muslim, just by looking at them. I was on a CNN debate recently with a profiling supporter who, when confronted with the facts, resorted to holding up the photos of the 19 hijackers of September 11, 2001, and insisting: "They all look alike."

The tragic shooting of Jean Charles de Menezes in the London subway[1] could have been based in part on his dress and behavior, as British authorities maintain. But almost certainly Menezes would not [have] been shot eight times in the head had he not been a young, brown-skinned man. British police looked at a Brazilian electrician and saw a Pakistani suicide-bomber.

Not that all the London bombers were of Pakistani origin—a fourth man was Jamaican. The failed bombers in the second group were all East Africans. And then you have Richard Reid,[2] John Walker Lindh[3] and Jose Padilla,[4] to mention but a few. But it's okay, "they all look alike."

Profiling Produces False Leads

Brooklyn Assemblyman Dov Hikind has also demanded that New York police use ethnic profiling in the subway searches, maintaining that "the London suicide bombers on July 7 and July 21 fit a very precise intelligence profile." He also found that "[T]hey all look a certain way." The police replied "racial profiling is illegal, of doubtful effectiveness, and against department policy."

Demagogues who call for profiling against American Muslims need to drop the pretense that this could be based on appearances or names. It would require Americans to

---

1. A Brazilian man living in London who was shot and killed by police who mistakenly thought he was a Muslim terrorist.
2. A British would-be terrorist.
3. A white American who was caught fighting with the Taliban in Afghanistan.
4. A New Yorker convicted of aiding terrorists.

Discrimination and Muslim Americans

Muslim Americans have reported experiencing increased discrimination since September 11, 2001.

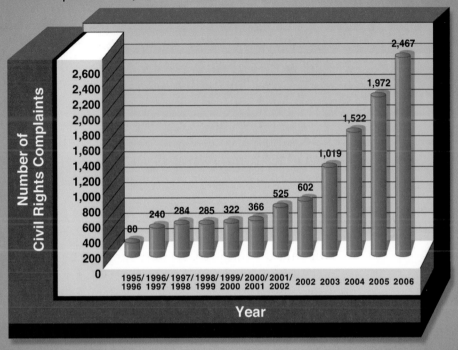

Taken from: "The Status of Muslim Civil Rights in the United States," Council on American-Islamic Relations, 2007, p. 5.

carry identity documents confirming their official religious designation. And even if it were possible to profile Arabs or Muslims by sight, or Muslims were forced to carry religious identification to be produced on demand, the effect would still be to cast an impossibly wide pool of suspects and distract attention from behavioral and other contingent factors that may actually point to a potential threat.

Race, ethnicity and religious affiliation, even when accurately identified, are widely recognized by law enforcement and counter-terrorism officials as false leads, which in themselves say nothing relevant about whether or not an individual may be about to commit a crime.

The U.S. government says that there was more evidence of intentional discrimination before September 11, 2001, than after.

Only two approaches in dealing with mass groups of people make sense: comprehensiveness, as at airports; or randomness, as in subways—anything in between serves less as a deterrent to terrorists and more as a tipping of the authorities' hand and a helpful hint for how not to get caught.

Profiling Did Not Prevent 9/11

When U.S. airport security was based on a supposedly neutral, secret computer profiling system, dating from 1996 and leading up to September 11, 2001, the evidence strongly suggested that it resulted in widespread discrimination against Arab and Muslim travelers. However, it did not prevent the September 11 attacks.

The intensified post–September 11 airport security regime has been both more thorough and more equitable, despite the ongoing bureaucratic nightmare of "no-fly" lists. There was more evidence of intentional discrimination against Arabs and Muslims in domestic air travel before September 11 than after, precisely because the U.S. government has had to accept that serious security threats require policies that do not boil down to crude stereotypes or rely on subjective judgments about ethnicity.

Toward the end of his tenure as the first secretary of homeland security, Tom Ridge, explained to Americans: "There was a legitimate concern right after 9/11 that the face of international terrorism was basically from the Middle East. We know differently. We don't have the luxury of kidding ourselves that there is an ethnic or racial or country profile."

Most Americans understand that fighting terrorism with racism is repugnant to their values and won't work. And most people have enough sense not to cut off their nose to spite their face. But not everyone.

Analyze the essay:

1. To make his argument, Ibish tells the story of Jean Charles de Menezes. Retell that story in your own words. Then, offer your thoughts on what the addition of Menezes's story lent to the essay's credibility and power.

2. The author of this essay, Hussein Ibish, is an Arab Muslim American. The author of the next essay, Michael Smerconish, is a white American. Does knowing the ethnicities of these two authors influence the way in which you read their arguments? If so, in what way?

Racially Profiling Arabs and Muslims Is Not Discriminatory

Michael Smerconish

In the following essay Michael Smerconish argues that racially profiling Arabs and Muslims is not discriminatory— it is commonsense police work that will help catch terrorists. He explains that the war on terror involves a very specific group of people who are very open about their intentions to harm Americans. It is foolish, says Smerconish, to ignore the fact that terrorists who attack America and its allies are most commonly Muslim and/or Arab. Profiling helps isolate these people, he claims, while other methods of screening, such as random searches, do not accurately apprehend criminals and inconvenience people who are least likely to be terrorists. Smerconish urges Americans to stop pretending that babies or marines might be terrorists. In his opinion, racial profiling is a justified means of catching terrorists and the best way to keep Americans safe.

Smerconish is the author of *Flying Blind: How Political Correctness Continues to Compromise Airline Safety Post 9/11* and *Muzzled: From T-Ball to Terrorism—True Stories That Should Be Fiction*.

Consider the following questions:
1. Name eight categories Smerconish says the terrorists who plotted to bring down planes over the Atlantic Ocean do *not* fit into.
2. Who do police typically question when seeking rapists, and what bearing does this have on Smerconish's argument?
3. Who is John Lehman, and what is he quoted as saying in this essay? What points do his statements support?

Michael Smerconish, "Profiling: Street Smarts by Any Other Name," Huffington Post.com, August 17, 2006. Reproduced by permission.

F ive years removed from 9/11, it's time to admit that "profiling" is not a dirty word. Profiling is street smarts by any other name. It's the common-sensical recognition that while America is not threatened by an entire community, she is under siege by a certain element of an identifiable group, and law enforcement needs to target its resources accordingly. . . .

Hopefully now there will be a long overdue confrontation of the Emperor Has No Clothes charade whereby law enforcement is mandated to ignore the nude barbarism of radical Islam. The arrest of two dozen in connection with the latest, failed plan [the 2006 terror plot to blow up airplanes over the Atlantic Ocean] should change that. After all, they are the same old, same old. I refer to Messrs. Ali, Ali, Ali, Hussain, Hussaind, Hussain, Islam, Kayani, Khan, Khan, Khatib, Patel, Rauf, Saddique, Sarwar, Savant Tariz, Uddin and Zaman. To a person they are Muslim men.

Where some would highlight the slight differences among them—class, upbringing and whether they were raised Muslim or converted to Islam—I see the commonalities. Equally significant is who they are not.

They are not Americans. They are not urban blacks. They are not suburban whites. They are not Jews. They are not Hispanics. They are not members of the U.S. military, women, senior citizens or young kids. At a minimum, it is time to profile by exclusion.

Tracking Suspicious People Makes Sense

Some are still standing in the way. Take Paul Stephenson, the Scotland Yard Deputy Commissioner, who, on the day the plot was made known, said:

"What I would want to say, and you would expect me to say about this, is this is not about communities. This is about criminals. This is about murderers; people who want to commit mass-murder. This is not about anything to do with any particular community."

Wrong, Deputy Stephenson, I would not expect you to say that. And while this is not about a particular community, it most certainly is about people within a particular community. More appropriate from London were the observations of Max Hastings in the *Daily Mail*. Hastings correctly noted "in every area of criminal activity, we accept that some people are more deserving than others of suspicion." He pointed out that police do not question women when seeking a rapist, don't round up short West Indians when pursuing a six foot white burglar, and don't arrest an elderly widow for car theft when security cameras captured an Asian male.

Random Screening Is Absurd

For years I have been advocating that the United States use this kind of street smarts in the war against radical Islam. I did not begin with any particular knowledge of the subject. To the contrary, whatever understanding I've obtained sprang from a common occurrence in connection with a routine flight.

In March of 2004, my family of six was heading to Florida for Spring break. At a ticket counter in the Atlantic City airport, my 8-year-old son was singled out for "secondary" or random screening.

I knew it was absurd, but I didn't complain, figuring it was the small price we all have to pay post 9/11. Common sense told me it was a terrible waste of precious resources.

Soon after my son's screening, Dr. Condoleezza Rice testified in front of the 9/11 Commission. Commissioner John Lehman floored me when he asked Dr. Rice this:

". . . were you aware that it was the policy, and I believe it remains the policy today, to fine airlines if they have more than two young Arab males in secondary questioning because that is discriminatory?"

I wondered what in the world he was talking about with his quota question. So I called Secretary Lehman and asked him. He told me that airline executives had said as much in testimony before the 9/11 Commission.

Lehman faulted political correctness and said "no one approves of racial profiling. That is not the issue, but the fact is that Norwegian women are not, and 85-year-old ladies with aluminum walkers are not, the source of the terrorist threat. And the fact is, our enemy is the violent Islamic extremism. And so the overwhelming number of people that one needs to worry about are young Arab males." . . .

Michael Smerconish, pictured, states that racial profiling against Arabs and Muslims is not discriminatory but commonsense police work to catch terrorists.

Profiling Has Caught Terrorists

What I have learned since 9/11 about the absence of profiling in America's war on Islamic fascism has filled two books that I have authored. Since 9/11 we have seen the Madrid train bombings, the Bali nightclub bombings, London bombings on 7/7 and the most recent threat of

a terror attack in the UK. My thesis remains unchanged. We are threatened by individuals who largely have race, gender, religion, ethnicity and appearance in common. To the extent we do not take that information into account as we seek to prevent a repeat of 9/11, we are still flying blind.

Among the more salient things that I have learned: . . .

We have profiling to thank for the fact that the presumed 20th hijacker was prevented from entering the United States. Mohammed al Khatani was denied entry on August 4, 2001 at the Orlando International Airport. Al Kahtani was then a Saudi national who came before a very alert secondary inspections officer named Jose Melendez-Perez. What caused Melendez-Perez to slow him down? As he told the 9/11 Commission about Kahtani, "he just gave me the creeps." Melendez-Perez was profiling, thank goodness. When he asked al Kahtani questions, the man's story didn't add up.

Racial Profiling Is Good Police Work

If I, an Arab immigrant, can come to terms with the fact that a limited use of racial profiling is necessary for the security of this country, then surely there is room in the national dialogue for those who stand up for our government's right to effectively protect its citizens.

Oubai Mohammad Shahbandar, "I'm an Arab; Profile Me," FrontPageMagazine.com, July 4, 2003.

Looks Are Everything

Michael Tuohey saw two of the hijackers on the morning of 9/11 and had the same instinct. Tuohey worked the ticket counter at the airport in Portland, Maine for US Airways. He'll never forget that particular day amongst his 34 years of employment. At 5:43 a.m. on a bright Tuesday morning, two men wearing sport coats and ties approached his ticket counter with just 17 minutes to spare before their flight to Boston. He thought this pair was unusual. "It was just the look on the one man's face, his eyes," Tuohey told me. In front of him were Mohamed Atta and Abdul Aziz al Omari.

"I looked up, and asked them the standard questions. The one guy was looking at me. It sent a chill through me. Something in my stomach churned. And subconsciously, I said to myself, 'if they don't look like Arab terrorists, nothing does.' Then I gave myself a mental slap. In over 34 years, I had checked in thousands of Arab travelers and I never thought this before. I said to myself, 'that's not nice to think. They are just two Arab businessmen," And with that, Tuohey handed them their boarding passes.

Atta and Omari arrived in Boston at 6:45 a.m., where they were joined by three accomplices. The five then checked in, and boarded American Airlines Flight No. 11 bound for L.A. At 8:46 a.m., it hit the North Tower. Now here is the irony. While Michael Tuohey will forever wonder what he should have done, the reality is that had he taken action, he would have been punished

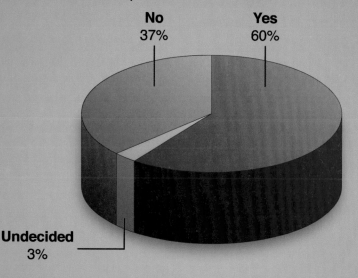

Americans Believe Muslims and Arabs Should Be Racially Profiled

A 2006 poll found the majority of Americans believe authorities should single out people who look "Middle Eastern" for security screening at locations such as airports and train stations.

No
37%

Yes
60%

Undecided
3%

Taken from: Quinnipiac University Polling Institute, 2006.

Jose Melendez-Perez, an inspection officer at Orlando International Airport, is credited with denying entry to Mohammed al Khatani, the alleged twentieth hijacker of September 11, 2001.

by our government just as our government fined United, American Airlines, Continental and Delta. . . .

It Makes Sense to Profile People Who Are Likely to Be Terrorists

Not only do we fail to single out certain individuals who bear commonalities with the terrorists, we do not excuse individuals from the process of secondary screening who so obviously do not deserve the scrutiny. From culling hundreds of emails and news accounts sent to me in the last five years, two incidents stand out, both with a Philadelphia connection. First, on May 3, 2006, three Marine honor guards were subject to secondary screening as they escorted the remains of a fallen comrade through the Philadelphia International Airport. How disgraceful.

Second is the case of the Yocum family from Boothwyn. Their experience occurred on October 28,

2002, at the Phoenix Sky Harbor International Airport. Claire Yocum delivered quadruplets 9 weeks premature. The babies then needed two months in the ICU. When they were finally able to fly home, they were selected for additional screening! Nineteen Arab look-alikes wreaked havoc on the U.S. on 9/11, and yet four newborns from Philadelphia are the ones getting the hairy eyeball. The babies, who were wrapped tight in blankets and had a net covering their car seats, were removed from their apparatus and searched. All of their bags, which were prepared and organized by nurses, had to be removed. In the process, the screeners woke the four sleeping babies.

I could go on and on.

Analyze the essay:

1. As part of his argument for why racial profiling is not discriminatory, Smerconish argues that Arabs and Muslims are a clearly identifiable group. In the previous essay, Hussein Ibish argued that Arabs and Muslims, who come from many different nations and cultures, cannot be identified by appearance. With which author do you ultimately agree? Why?

2. This viewpoint used narrative elements to make its point that racial profiling is not discriminatory. Identify these narrative elements and explain whether they helped convince you of the author's argument.

Affirmative Action Helps Correct Discrimination

Coalition to Defend Affirmative Action, Integration & Immigrant Rights and Fight for Equality by Any Means Necessary (BAMN)

The following essay is written by the Coalition to Defend Affirmative Action, Integration & Immigrant Rights and Fight for Equality by Any Means Necessary (BAMN). In it, the authors argue that because America continues to practice discrimination against minorities and women, qualified students need affirmative action to be fairly and equally represented at America's colleges and universities. They argue that affirmative action helps open doors for people who have otherwise been denied such opportunities and as such is a fair and necessary policy. Furthermore, they contend that affirmative action is not a "free ride"—it does not allow unqualified people to be accepted into a school, it just gives disadvantaged people the chance to be noticed in the applicant pool. Also, they suggest that more diverse schools offer a better learning environment because they are composed of people who bring different skills and experiences to the table. The authors conclude that affirmative action helps end discrimination and creates new opportunities for people who have led disadvantaged lives. As long as sexism and racism continue to exist, they argue, affirmative action policies are needed.

Coalition to Defend Affirmative Action, Integration & Immigrant Rights and Fight for Equality by Any Means Necessary (BAMN), "Lies and Misinformation Used to Attack Affirmative Action," www.bamn.com, October 1, 2006. Reproduced by permission.

Consider the following questions:

1. Explain the *Grutter v. Bollinger* court case, as described by the authors.
2. According to the authors, black students make up what percent of the University of Michigan student body? How does this compare to the black college-age population of Michigan as a whole?
3. Who do the authors say are like "arsonists lecturing the fire department"?

The rightwingers say they are for a "meritocracy" and that eliminating affirmative action will help achieve that aim.

The truth . . .

The actual effect of [reversing affirmative action] would be to exclude the majority of fully qualified black, Latina/o and Native American students from admission to the University of Michigan and other colleges and universities in our state. *That is not "meritocracy".* It would resegregate the University of Michigan. In the *Grutter v. Bollinger* trial, all sides conceded that *all the minority students admitted into the University of Michigan Law School were fully qualified.* Even the anti–affirmative action lawyers who sued the University of Michigan in the name of Jennifer Gratz and Barbara Grutter conceded that these fully qualified minority students would be barred without affirmative action admissions programs. Without affirmative action, institutional inequality stifles merit.

Increasing Inequality

The rightwingers promoting the initiative to outlaw all affirmative action for women and minorities say that they are for equality.

Pro–affirmative action supporters march in front of the U.S. Supreme Court Building.

Outlawing affirmative action programs *will increase inequality*—between women and men and between the races. Treat people equally from day one and you will not need anti-discrimination remedies like affirmative action. Patterns of discrimination operate unchecked in the absence of active policies like affirmative action. Affirmative action is a step toward fairness and a step in the direction of judging people on the basis of "merit" by offsetting the unfair disadvantage that comes with not being white and male in our society.

Racism is a reality. Sexism is a reality. As long as racism and sexism exist, we will need active policies like affirmative action to offset the damage they do.

Affirmative Action Levels the Playing Field

The rightwingers say that everyone should be treated the same.

We must start with reality. Both bias and unearned privilege exist today; pretending that this is not true and outlawing the policies designed to offset that problem would simply exacerbate an already very bad problem. Race would be a much greater factor in college admissions and in our society as a whole if affirmative action were outlawed.

Black students are still dramatically underrepresented at the University of Michigan even with affirmative action in place. Black students are less than 6% of the U of M student body, while the college-aged population of Michigan is almost 20% black. We have not yet achieved equal opportunity in American education. We must move forward; this petition will take us backward toward segregation.

Affirmative Action Benefits Everyone, Even Whites

[Some people say,] "I support affirmative action just not 'racial preferences'".

That's a lie. The same ballot language in Ward Connerly's California Proposition 209, which passed in 1996, *outlawed all affirmative action—including outreach programs!* "Racial preferences" is just the racists' term for the programs that offset the real preference this society shows white people and men every day.

[Some people say,] "I support socio-economic affirmative action not race-based affirmative action."

Counterposing race-based affirmative action with socioeconomic affirmative action is just the racists' way of sounding less elitist. Poor and working class white people, both men and women, have benefited from affirmative action policies. The affirmative action program that Jennifer Gratz forced the University of Michigan to

---

Affirmative Action Helps Individuals

The United States is a system built upon the backbreaking labor, systematic abuse, and marginalization of people of color, women, and other subordinate groups. Affirmative action is a program that seeks to provide equity for these marginalized groups. It helps to create a balance against the white supremacist patriarchy in which we live.

Eric Stoller, "Affirmative Action," Ericstoller. com, March 4, 2006. http://ericstoller.com/ blog/2006/03/04/affirmative-action/.

A History of Affirmative Action Policies in America

1961	Affirmative action is used for the first time when President John F. Kennedy signs Executive Order (E.O.) 10925, which instructed federal contractors to take "affirmative action to ensure that applicants are treated equally without regard to race, color, religion, sex, or national origin." The Committee on Equal Employment Opportunity is created.
1964	The Civil Rights Act of 1964 becomes law. It prohibits employment discrimination by large employers (over 15 employees). The Equal Opportunity Commission (EEOC) is established.
1965	President Lyndon B. Johnson issues E.O. 11246, which requires all government contractors and subcontractors to take affirmative action to expand job opportunities for minorities.
1967	E.O. 11246 is expanded to include affirmative action for women.
1970	The Labor Department, under President Richard M. Nixon, issues Order No. 4, which authorizes flexible goals and timetables to correct "underutilization" of minorities by federal contractors.
1971	Order No. 4 is revised to include women.
1971	President Nixon issues E.O. 11625, which directs federal agencies to develop plans and program goals for a national Minority Business Enterprise (MBE) contracting program.
1978	The U.S. Supreme Court in *Regents of the University of California v. Bakke* upholds the use of race as one factor in choosing among qualified applicants for admission. At the same time, it also rules that the University Medical School's practice of reserving 18 seats in each entering class of 100 for disadvantaged minority students is unlawful.
1979	President Jimmy Carter issues E.O. 12138, creating a National Women's Business Enterprise Policy and requiring each agency to take affirmative action to support women's business enterprises.
1979	The Supreme Court in *United Steel Workers of America, AFL-CIO v. Weber* rules that race-conscious affirmative action efforts designed to eliminate a conspicuous racial imbalance in a employer's workforce resulting from past discrimination are permissible if they are temporary and do not violate the rights of white employees.
1983	President Ronald Reagan issues E.O. 12432, which directs each federal agency with grant-making authority to develop a Minority Business Enterprise (MBE) developmental plan.
1986	The Supreme Court in *Local 128 of the Sheet Metal Workers' International Association v. EEOC* upholds a judicially ordered 29% minority "membership admission goal" for a union that had intentionally discriminated against minorities, confirming that courts may order race-conscious relief to correct and prevent future discrimination.
1987	The Supreme Court rules in *Johnson v. Transportation Agency, Santa Clara County, California,* that a severe under representation of women and minorities justified the use of race or sex as "one factor" in choosing among qualified candidates.

1994	In *Adarand Constructors, Inc. v. Peña* the Supreme Court rules that a federal affirmative action program is constitutional when narrowly tailored to accomplish a compelling government interest such as remedying discrimination.
1995	President Bill Clinton declares his support for affirmative action programs by announcing his administration's policy of "Mend it, don't end it."
1995	The Regents of the University of California vote to end affirmative action programs at all University of California campuses. Beginning in 1997 for graduate schools and 1998 for undergraduate admissions, officials at the university are no longer allowed to use race, gender, ethnicity, or national origin as a factor in admissions decisions.
1996	California's Proposition 209 passes by a narrow margin. It abolishes all public-sector affirmative action programs in the state in employment, education, and contracting.
1996	In *Texas v. Hopwood* the U.S. Court of Appeals for the Fifth Circuit rules against the University of Texas, deciding that its law school's policy of considering race in the admissions process was a violation of the Constitution's equal-protection guarantee.
1997	Lawsuits are filed against the University of Michigan and the University of Washington School of Law regarding their use of affirmative action policies in admissions standards.
1998	Both the United States House of Representatives and the United States Senate thwart attempts to eliminate specific affirmative action programs.
1998	As a result of the ban on use of affirmative action in admissions at the University of California, UC Berkeley experiences a 61% drop in admissions of African American, Latino/a, and Native American students, and UCLA has a 36% decline.
1998	Voters in Washington pass Initiative 200, which bans affirmative action in higher education, public contracting, and hiring.
2000	The Florida legislature passes "One Florida" Plan, banning affirmative action.
2000	In an effort to promote equal pay, the U.S. Department of Labor for the first time in history requires federal contractors to report hiring, termination, promotions, and compensation data by minority status and gender.
2002	The Sixth Circuit decides in *Grutter v. Bollinger* that it is constitutional for race to be used as one of many factors in admissions decisions at the University of Michigan's Law School.
2003	The Supreme Court makes rulings in *Grutter v. Bollinger* and *Gratz v. Bollinger*. In *Grutter*, the Court holds it is constitutional for race to be used as one of many factors in admissions decisions at the University of Michigan's Law School. However, in *Gratz*, the Court rejects the point-based affirmative action system at the College of Literature, Science and the Arts.
2006	In *Parents v. Seattle* and *Meredith v. Jefferson* the Supreme Court decides diversity programs in Seattle and Louisville, Kentucky, are unconstitutional.

Taken from: "Chronology: All (1775 thru 2005) Affirmative Action has been used since 1961 to expand opportunity and promote equality," Americans for a Fair Chance, August 15, 2008. Copyright © 2008 Leadership Conference on Civil Rights/Leadership Conference on Civil Rights Education Fund. All rights reserved. Reproduced by permission.

Ward Connerly's California Proposition 209 outlawed all affirmative action and outreach programs. The proposition was highly controversial.

abandon included socioeconomic affirmative action. After the ban on affirmative action in California in 1996, the mean family income of the student body at UC Berkeley increased, demonstrating that only wealthier students were being admitted.

When Affirmative Action Is No Longer Needed, It Will No Longer Be Used

[Some people say,] "The real problem is K–12 education."

K–12 education in America is segregated and unequal. Resegregating higher education will make that much worse and will move our whole society backward toward more segregation and more marginalization of minorities. The same rightwing forces attempting to ban affirmative action in higher education are attempting to ban all desegregation programs in K–12 schools. People attempting to justify their campaign to outlaw integration programs for higher education by talking about the inequality in K–12 play the part of arsonists lecturing the fire department. With people like this hypocrisy knows no limits.

[Some people say,] "Affirmative action has created a stigma of inferiority for its beneficiaries."

The stigma of inferiority comes from the discrimination, prejudice and inequality that necessitate affirmative action, not from affirmative action itself. Before affirmative action existed, there was much more stigma than there is now. The stigma comes from the racist misconception that black, Latina/o and Native American people are inferior to white people.

Analyze the essay:

1. In this essay the authors argue that because discrimination is still a feature of American life, affirmative action policies are needed to level the playing field. How do you think each of the other authors in this section might respond to this suggestion? List each speaker, and write two or three sentences on what you think their response might be.
2. To prove that current admissions policies are biased, BAMN shows the difference between the black student population of Michigan and the black student population at the University of Michigan. In your opinion, is this a strong piece of evidence? Should a state school's student body mirror the state's population demographics? Why or why not?

Affirmative Action Hurts Those It Is Intended to Help

Richard H. Sander

In the following essay Richard H. Sander explains why he believes affirmative action does not correct discrimination. He claims that affirmative action policies place black students at schools they are not truly qualified for. As a result, they are more likely to rank low in their classes, get poorer grades, flunk exit and professional exams, and drop out of school entirely. In this way, affirmative action hurts their self-esteem and career goals. Sander claims that merit-based admissions, on the other hand, would actually increase the number of skilled black professionals in fields such as law. He concludes that color-blind admissions policies are the best way to counter discrimination and disadvantage in student populations.

Sander is a law professor at the University of California at Los Angeles.

Consider the following questions:

1. What effect does the author say affirmative action has had on black students at Ivy League schools who planned to have an academic career?
2. How much more likely are black students to drop out of law school than white students, according to Sander? What explanation does he give for this?
3. What is the "mismatch effect," as described by Sander?

Richard H. Sander, "Affirmative action hurts those it's supposed to help," *Pittsburgh Tribune-Review*, January 2, 2005. Reproduced by permission of the author.

Traditionally, critics of affirmative action have focused either on its unfairness to those groups that don't receive preferences (usually whites and Asians) or on the inherent conflict between racial preferences and the legal ideal of color-blindness.

Over the last few years, however, a new and potentially even more damaging line of inquiry has emerged—the idea that racial preferences may materially harm the very people they are intended to benefit.

For instance, researchers Stephen Cole and Elinor Barber found that racial preferences at Ivy League colleges had a large and negative effect on the academic aspirations of black students.

The mechanism worked like this: Blacks admitted to elite schools with large preferences had more trouble competing with their classmates, and tended to get lower grades. Low grades, in turn, sapped the confidence of students, persuading them that they would not be able to compete effectively in Ph.D. programs. As a result, blacks at Ivy League schools were only half as likely as blacks at state universities to stick with plans for an academic career.

Dartmouth psychologist Rogers Elliot and three co-authors found that the same problem was keeping blacks out of the sciences.

Black students who received preferential admissions were at such a strong academic disadvantage compared with their classmates that fully half of those interested in the sciences tended to switch to majors with easier grading and less competition. Again, the net effect of preferential policies was to "mismatch" blacks with their academic environments.

My research over the last two years, using recent data that track more than 30,000 law students and lawyers, has documented even more serious and pervasive mismatch effects in legal education.

A student does her homework on the campus of Princeton University. Researchers found that Ivy League colleges' racial preferences had a negative effect on academic aspirations of black students.

Elite law schools offer very substantial racial preferences for blacks, Hispanics and American Indians in order to create student bodies that are as racially diverse as their applicant pools. Because these elite schools admit the black students that second-tier law schools would normally admit, second-tier schools, to keep up their minority numbers, also offer big racial preferences. The result is a cascade effect down the law school hierarchy, leaving 80 percent to 90 percent of black students at significantly more selective schools than they would get into strictly on their academic credentials.

Most legal educators have traditionally assumed that this helps blacks by giving them a more elite degree, better connections and maybe even a better education.

But in fact, my data show, about half of black law students end up in the bottom tenth of their classes. Very low grades lead to much higher attrition (blacks are 2 1/2 times more likely to drop out of law school than whites) and to more trouble on the bar exam (blacks are six times as likely as whites taking the bar to never pass).

The other traditional justification for racial preferences by law schools was that they would increase the number of black lawyers. But over the years the pool of black applicants has become much larger and much more qualified. More than 85 percent of blacks admitted to law schools today would still get into some law school if preferences disappeared—albeit generally a lower-prestige school.

The modest pool-expanding effects of law school preferences may well be more than canceled out now by the greater attrition caused by the mismatch effect. My research suggests that in a race-blind system, the proportion of black law students graduating and passing the bar on their first attempt would rise from 45 percent to at least 65 percent, and the number of new, certified black lawyers each year would rise about 7 percent.

Obviously, it's difficult to predict how applicants would weigh the pluses and minuses of a race-neutral system; the point is that the attrition effects of the current system are so devastating that they threaten all its intended benefits.

> ## Affirmative Action Hurts Those It Is Supposed to Help
>
> By lowering academic qualifications for Blacks, it inevitably sends a message that Blacks can't be expected to compete intellectually with other groups. This reinforces the stereotype of Black intellectual inferiority—that Blacks can't possibly be held to the same academic standard as Whites or Asians.
>
> Roger Clegg, "African Americans Should Oppose Racial Preferences," *Black Issues in Higher Education*, vol. 20, no. 25, January 29, 2004, p. 74.

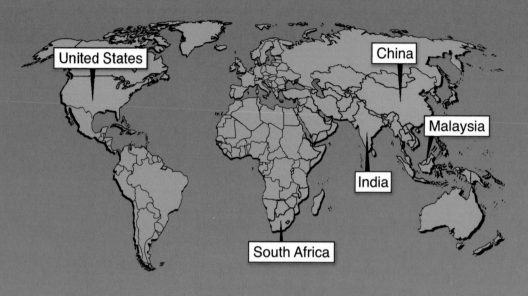

Affirmative Action Around the World

Only a handful of the world's countries have affirmative action policies.

United States

China

Malaysia

India

South Africa

Taken from: Reuters, April 10, 2008.

All of this doesn't prove, by any means, that affirmative action is harmful in every form. Some recent research by Princeton sociologist Marta Tienda found, for example, that although minority preferences at elite undergraduate colleges had a harmful effect on grades, these effects were more than offset by the success of those schools in helping students graduate. Improving academic support programs in law schools would certainly help narrow black-white grade gaps up to a point.

And my research suggests that shrinking law school racial preferences by half—that is, moving the standards for blacks and minorities closer to the standards for whites and Asians—would reduce by three-quarters the attrition effects I document.

The affirmative action debate has generally been characterized by two camps that resolutely see the other side as hopelessly misguided or even evil. Social scientists entering the fray have tended to become partisan spokespersons for one side or the other. The

Whether racial preferences ultimately help or hurt minority students is an ongoing matter of debate.

emergence of careful, credible research on the mismatch effect may lead us to a more measured debate on when preferences produce clear net benefits and about how quickly we can move toward what everyone agrees is the ultimate goal—color-blind admissions.

Analyze the essay:

1. In this essay Richard H. Sander uses studies, facts, and examples to argue against affirmative action policies. He does not, however, use any quotations to support his point. If you were to rewrite this article and insert quotations, what authorities might you quote from? Where would you place these quotations to bolster the points Sander makes?

2. Sander suggests that affirmative action policies mismatch students with schools, placing them at institutions for which they are not truly qualified. How do you think the authors of the previous essay, the Coalition to Defend Affirmative Action, Integration & Immigrant Rights and Fight for Equality by Any Means Necessary (BAMN), would respond to that suggestion?

Section Two:
Model Essays
and Writing
Exercises

The Five-Paragraph Essay

An *essay* is a short piece of writing that discusses or analyzes one topic. The five-paragraph essay is a form commonly used in school assignments and tests. Every five-paragraph essay begins with an *introduction*, ends with a *conclusion*, and features three *supporting paragraphs* in the middle.

The Thesis Statement. The introduction includes the essay's thesis statement. The thesis statement presents the argument or point the author is trying to make about the topic. The essays in this book all have different thesis statements because they are making different arguments about discrimination.

The thesis statement should clearly tell the reader what the essay will be about. A focused thesis statement helps determine what will be in the essay; the subsequent paragraphs are spent developing and supporting its argument.

The Introduction. In addition to presenting the thesis statement, a well-written introductory paragraph captures the attention of the reader and explains why the topic being explored is important. It may provide the reader with background information on the subject matter or feature an anecdote that illustrates a point relevant to the topic. It could also present startling information that clarifies the point of the essay or put forth a contradictory position that the essay will refute. Further techniques for writing an introduction are found later in this section.

The Supporting Paragraphs. The introduction is then followed by three (or more) supporting paragraphs. These are the main body of the essay. Each paragraph presents and develops a *subtopic* that supports the essay's thesis statement. Each subtopic is spearheaded by a *topic sentence* and supported by its own facts, details, and examples. The writer can use various kinds of supporting material and details to back up the topic of each supporting paragraph. These may include statistics, quotations from people with special knowledge or expertise, historic facts, and anecdotes. A rule of writing is that specific and concrete examples are more convincing than vague, general, or unsupported assertions.

The Conclusion. The conclusion is the paragraph that closes the essay. Its function is to summarize or reiterate the main idea of the essay. It may recall an idea from the introduction or briefly examine the larger implications of the thesis. Because the conclusion is also the last chance a writer has to make an impression on the reader, it is important that it not simply repeat what has been presented elsewhere in the essay but close it in a clear, final, and memorable way.

Although the order of the essay's component paragraphs is important, they do not have to be written in the order presented here. Some writers like to decide on a thesis and write the introduction paragraph first. Other writers like to focus first on the body of the essay and write the introduction and conclusion later.

Pitfalls to Avoid

When writing essays about controversial issues such as discrimination, it is important to remember that disputes over the material are common precisely because there are many different perspectives. Remember to state your arguments in careful and measured terms. Evaluate your topic fairly—avoid overstating negative qualities of one perspective or understating positive qualities of another. Use examples, facts, and details to support any assertions you make.

The Narrative Essay

Narrative writing is writing that tells a story or describes an event. Stories are something most people are familiar with since childhood. When you describe what you did on your summer vacation, you are telling a story. Journalists write stories of yesterday's events. Novelists write fictional stories about imagined events.

Stories are often found in essays meant to persuade. The previous section of this book provided you with examples of essays about discrimination. Most are persuasive essays that attempt to convince the reader to support specific arguments about discrimination. In addition to making arguments, some of the authors of these essays also tell stories in which discrimination plays a part. They used narrative writing to do this.

Components of Narrative Writing

All stories contain basic components of *characters, setting,* and *plot.* These components answer four basic questions—who, when, where, and what—that readers need to make sense of the story being told.

Characters answer the question of whom the story is about. In a personal narrative using the first-person perspective ("My boss discriminated against me when handing out promotions"), the characters are the writer and the boss. But writers can also tell the story of other people or characters ("Sarah Smith knew profiling was wrong, but she couldn't help feeling it was the only way to catch terrorists") without being part of the story themselves.

The *setting* answers the questions of when and where the story takes place. The more details given about characters and setting, the more the reader learns about them and the author's views toward them. In Viewpoint Three, author Hussein Ibish describes the London subway as the setting of the shooting of Jean Charles de Menezes. Model Essay Two describes the setting in more detail, but both versions give the reader an idea of where the story takes place.

The *plot* answers the question of what happens to the characters. It often involves conflict or obstacles that a story's character confronts and must somehow resolve. An example is found in Model Essay Three in this book, which tells the story of a Jewish woman who is verbally assaulted and intimidated by a prejudiced grocery clerk. How the grocery clerk chooses to act and how the narrator chooses to respond affect the outcome of the story.

Some people distinguish narrative essays from stories in that narrative essays have a point—that is, in addition to telling a story, there is a general observation, argument, or insight that the author wants to impress upon the reader. In other words, narrative essays also answer "why" questions: Why did these particular events happen to the character? Why is this story worth retelling? What can be learned from this story? Why is it important? The story's point is the essay's thesis. For example, Viewpoint Four by Michael Smerconish uses the story of the Yocum family to make the point that randomly screening airport passengers is not a good way to catch terrorists. He does not explicitly say this, but his point that racial profiling is effective is clear from the way he tells the Yocum family's story.

Using Narrative Writing in Persuasive Essays

Narrative writing can be used in persuasive essays in several different ways. Stories can be used in the introductory paragraph(s) to grab the reader's attention and to introduce the thesis. Stories can comprise all or part of the middle paragraphs that are used to support the thesis. They may even be used in concluding paragraphs as a way to restate and reinforce the essay's general point. Narrative essays may focus on one particular story, such as Model Essay One, which focuses on the story of Shania Eldridge. Or, like Viewpoint Four, which spotlights the stories of the Yocum family, Mohammed al Khatani, Michael Tuohey, Mohamed Atta, Abdul Aziz al Omari, and Michael Smerconish's own family, narrative essays may draw upon multiple stories to make their point.

A narrative story can also be used as one of several arguments or supporting points. Or, a narrative can take up an entire essay. Some stories are used as just one of several pieces of evidence that an author offers to make a point. In this type of essay, the author usually writes a formal conclusion that ties together for the reader the connection between the story and the point of the essay. In other narrative essays, the story discussed is so powerful that by the time the reader reaches the end of the narrative, the author's main point is clear, and they need not offer a formal conclusion.

In the following section, you will read some model essays on discrimination that use narrative writing. You will also do exercises that will help you write your own narrative essays.

America's Wage Gap: Paying Women Less than Men

Editor's Notes As you read in Preface A, narrative writing has several uses. In the real world, writers may incorporate the narrative technique into another type of essay, such as a persuasive or a cause-effect essay. They may also choose to use narrative only in portions of their essay. Instead of focusing their whole essay on a single story, they may use several different stories together.

This is the structure of the following model essay: It uses pieces of narration to discuss discrimination against women. As you read, pay attention to the essay's components and how they are organized. Also note that all sources are cited using Modern Language Association (MLA) style.* For more information on how to cite your sources see Appendix C. In addition, consider the following:

1. How does the introduction engage the reader's attention?
2. How is narration used in the essay?
3. What purpose do the essay's quotes serve?
4. Would the essay be as effective if it contained only general arguments and the story of Shania Eldridge had not been included?

■ Refers to thesis and topic sentences

■ Refers to supporting details

Paragraph 1

Most people are surprised to learn that in the twenty-first century, American women continue to be paid less than men for doing the same job with the same credentials, education, and experience. According to the U.S. Census Bureau, women are paid approximately seventy-seven

The introduction should grab the reader's attention and make him or her curious to know more. Did this happen to you while reading this introduction?

---

* Editor's Note: In applying MLA style guidelines in this book, the following simplifications have been made: Parenthetical text citations are confined to direct quotations only; electronic source documentation in the Works Cited list omits date of access, page ranges, and some detailed facts of publication.

cents for every dollar a man is paid. That hard-working, well-educated women continue to be paid less than men is an outrageous injustice that Americans must correct immediately.

Paragraph 2

Consider the case of Shania Eldridge, a thirty-one-year-old banker from Baton Rouge, Louisiana. Eldridge makes about 25 percent less than the men who work in her bank, despite the fact that she holds a similar level position and has been employed there for a similar amount of time. Economist Evelyn Murphy, president and founder of the WAGE Project, which tracks the differences of pay between men and women, estimates the wage gap costs a woman like Eldridge between $700,000 and $2 million over the course of her working lifetime. Women of color suffer from the wage gap even more— it is reported that African American women earn only sixty-eight cents, and Latinas fifty-seven cents, for every dollar that men earn. Asian American and Pacific Islander American women are statistically the best earners of all women but still earn only eighty-eight cents for every dollar that men earn.

Paragraph 3

The fact that Eldridge has a college degree and previous banking experience has not helped close the wage gap in her field. This is perhaps one of the most alarming aspects of the wage gap: that it is not the result of women being less qualified or less educated than their male counterparts. For more than twenty-five years, women have accounted for the majority of the nation's college students (58 percent of college students were women and just 42 percent were men in 2006). And a 2007 study by the American Association of University Women found that even just one year after college graduation, women like Eldridge earn just 80 percent of what men do. Eldridge is particularly disadvantaged because she happens to live in a state with a larger pay disparity—according to a 2007 study, Virginia (in addition to Louisiana, New Jersey, Indiana, and South Carolina) ranks among the states with the biggest pay disparities, where women over twenty-five earn only approximately 64 percent of what their male counterparts do. Women in West Virginia and Washington, DC, earn more, about 89 percent of what men do—but that is still not equal pay.

What point in Paragraph 3 does this statistic support?

Paragraph 4

There are several explanations for why Eldridge and women like her continue to suffer unequal pay for equal work. First, long-held, ongoing assumptions that men are better suited for jobs that involve leadership, decision making, finances, and business continue to prevail in many sectors of the workforce. Second, female workers who are of child-bearing age are at a disadvantage when they are applying for a job, as employers may be reluctant to hire someone who is likely to go on maternity leave. (Though the law says they cannot discriminate on this basis, it is often hard to enforce.) Finally, even when a woman does get the job, she usually receives discriminatory working conditions and unequal supplies. For example, after studying the treatment of female and male employees, the Massachusetts Institute of Technology found its female scientists were routinely given less pay, space, funding, and rewards than their male colleagues. "Did anyone intentionally give them smaller offices and labs? Probably not," says Heidi Hartmann, president of the Institute for Women's Policy Research. "It's just one of those things [that] accumulate and add up to barriers and institutional discrimination" (qtd. in Sahadi).

This is the topic sentence of Paragraph 4. It is a subset of the essay's thesis. It tells what specific point this paragraph will be about.

"First," "Second," and "Finally," are all transitional phrases. These kinds of phrases keep the ideas in the paragraph connected and moving forward.

Note how this quote supports the ideas discussed in the paragraph. It also comes from a reputable source.

Paragraph 5

Shania Eldridge is just one woman who will miss out on thousands of dollars over the course of her lifetime simply because she is a woman. The discrimination against American women in the workplace is an embarrassment to a society that claims to value equality, not to mention

Note how the essay's conclusion wraps up the topic in a final, memorable way—without repeating all the points made in the essay.

one that is 51 percent female. Women and men must work together to correct this injustice, because a United States that pays everyone what he or she is worth is a better, prouder country.

Works Cited

Sahadi, Jeanne. "The 76-Cent Myth: Do Women Make Less than Men?" CNN.com 21 Feb. 2006 < http://money.cnn.com/2006/02/21/commentary/everyday/sahadi/ > .

Exercise 1A: Create an Outline from an Existing Essay

It often helps to create an outline of the five-paragraph essay before you write it. The outline can help you organize the information, arguments, and evidence you have gathered during your research.

For this exercise, create an outline that could have been used to write Model Essay One: "America's Wage Gap: Paying Women Less than Men." This "reverse engineering" exercise is meant to help familiarize you with how outlines can help classify and arrange information.

To do this you will need to

1. articulate the essay's thesis,
2. pinpoint important pieces of evidence,
3. flag quotes that supported the essay's idea, and
4. identify key points that supported the argument.

Part of the outline has already been started to give you an idea of the assignment.

Outline

I. Paragraph 1

Write the essay's thesis: That hard-working, well-educated women continue to be paid less than men is an outrageous injustice that must be corrected.

II. Paragraph 2

Topic:

Supporting Detail i: Statistic from The WAGE Project estimating that the wage gap costs a woman between $700,000 and $2 million over the course of her working lifetime.

Supporting Detail ii:

III. Paragraph 3
Topic: An alarming aspect of the wage gap is that it is not the result of women being less qualified or educated than their male counterparts.

  i. Over the last 25 years, more American women have gone to college than men.

  ii.

IV. Paragraph 4
Topic:

  i.

  ii. Quote from Heidi Hartmann about inequity in the workplace.

V. Paragraph 5
  i. Write the essay's conclusion:

Exercise 1B: Create an Outline for Your Own Essay

The first model essay expresses a particular point of view about discrimination. For this exercise, your assignment is to find supporting ideas, choose specific and concrete details, create an outline, and ultimately write a five-paragraph essay making a different, even opposing, point about discrimination. Your goal is to use narrative techniques to convince your reader.

Part I: Write a thesis statement.

The following thesis statement would be appropriate for an opposing narrative essay on the wage gap:

> *The wage gap is not usually the result of discrimination, but rather the result of different choices made by women and men throughout their careers.*

Or see the sample paper topics suggested in Appendix D for more ideas.

Part II: Brainstorm pieces of supporting evidence

Using information found in this book and from your own research, write down three arguments or pieces of evidence that support the thesis statement you selected. Then, for each of these three arguments, write down facts, examples, and details that support it. These could be

- statistical information;
- personal memories and anecdotes;
- quotes from experts, peers, or family members;
- observations of people's actions and behaviors;
- specific and concrete details.

Supporting pieces of evidence for the above sample thesis statement might include:

- The fact that women tend to take off months or years of work to raise children drastically cuts into the amount they are able to earn over the course of their lives. See the facts in Appendix A of this book that support this. According to the National Center for Public Analysis, working mothers are nearly twice as likely to take time off to care for their children as are working fathers in two-income families. According to the center, when women behave in the workplace as men do, the wage gap between them is small.
- Research presented in the book *Women Don't Ask: Negotiation and the Gender Divide* by Linda Babcock and Sara Laschever. Babcock and Laschever point

out that salaries are determined by negotiations, and men tend to initiate negotiations four times more often than women do and ask for more money when they do so.

- Research presented in the book *Why Men Earn More: The Startling Truth Behind the Pay Gap—and What Women Can Do About It* by Warren Farrell. Farrell argues that men are more likely than women to sign up for tasks that directly increase their paycheck, such as relocating, traveling, taking on jobs that involve financial risk and reward, and working under unpleasant, messy, or dangerous conditions.

Part III: Place the information from Parts I and II in outline form.

Part IV: Write the arguments or supporting statements in paragraph form.

By now you have three arguments that support the essay's thesis statement, as well as supporting material. Use the outline to write out your three supporting arguments in paragraph form. Be sure each paragraph has a topic sentence that states the paragraph's thesis clearly and broadly. Then, add sentences that express the facts, quotes, details, and examples that support the paragraph's argument. The paragraph may also have a concluding or summary sentence.

Why Racial Profiling
Does Not Work

Essay
Two

Editor's Notes The following piece of writing is another persuasive essay that uses narrative techniques to make its point. It tells the story of Jean Charles de Menezes, a Brazilian man who was the victim of racial profiling. The characters, setting, and plot are recounted in more detail than they would be in a simple anecdote in order to better engage the reader in the story. In this way the author relies on the power of the story itself to make the essay's point that racial profiling is a discriminatory practice that is not an effective law enforcement technique.

The notes in the margins provide questions that will help you analyze how this essay is organized and written.

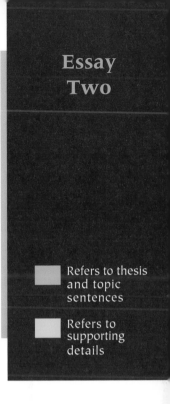

Refers to thesis and topic sentences

Refers to supporting details

Paragraph 1

Racial profiling—the process of using a person's racial or ethnic qualities to determine whether he or she is a suspect—is a controversial police technique that should be eliminated from law enforcement's playbook. Not only is racial profiling discriminatory, but its use often results in poor police work. When suspects are investigated because of their race or ethnicity, officers tend to reach sloppy and erroneous conclusions, oftentimes while the real perpetrator gets away. The story of Jean Charles de Menezes illustrates all the problems with racial profiling and is another example in which an innocent man paid the ultimate price as a result of discriminatory racial profiling practices.

This is the essay's thesis statement. How do you know it will feature narrative techniques?

Paragraph 2

In the summer of 2005, all of London was on edge. On July 7, four suicide terrorists detonated bombs inside the London subway system, the Tube, killing fifty-two people. The bombers, British Muslims who claimed the attacks were retribution for Britain's involvement in the war in Iraq, put bombs in backpacks and blended in with the other passengers of London's Tube trains. Just two weeks later, on July 21, London seemed under the threat of attack again when bombs were found in another Tube station. It was eventually determined that these bombs were fakes, designed to be a hoax—but they added to the nerves and high-running tensions in the country.

Paragraph 2 develops the story's setting. What kinds of details do you learn about the context in which the murder of Menezes occurred?

Paragraph 3

This is the topic sentence of Paragraph 3. Without reading the rest of the paragraph, guess what the paragraph will be about.

It was in this context that a twenty-seven-year-old man named Jean Charles de Menezes was gunned down by police using racial profiling to catch terrorists. Police initially said Menezes seemed suspicious because he was wearing a bulky, heavy jacket on a warm summer day. When they called to him, he reportedly ran away from them, furthering their suspicions. Also, police took his tan complexion to mean he was Arab or Southeast Asian, two groups of people that have repeatedly been associated with terrorism.

Paragraph 4

Only later did police learn that Menezes was a twenty-seven-year-old electrician from Brazil with no connections to al Qaeda or any other terrorist group. The heavy jacket he was reportedly wearing turned out to be a light jean jacket, perfectly appropriate attire for summer in London. Police also later retracted their claim that Menezes was running away from them—in fact, he was shot while sitting calmly on the train. Despite the fact that Menezes was a perfectly normal, unsuspicious man just trying to get somewhere on the Tube, police profiled him as a potential terrorist and shot him eight times in the head without even a question asked. There is no doubt that Menezes was killed as a result of discriminatory racial profiling policies. As one observer put it, "Tensions were high at the time, but his shooting occurred in part because of his darker complexion. Last I checked, Brazil was in South America, not the Middle East. Things get

What details have been included? How do they help you picture all the elements of the story?

What point does this quote support?

confusing when entire communities become targets of suspicion and, inevitably, innocents suffer." (Green) Furthermore, Green makes the excellent point that there is nothing to stop al Qaeda from getting around racial profiling practices simply by recruiting operatives who do not look Middle Eastern.

Paragraph 5

Jean Charles de Menezes is a classic case of why racial profiling does not work—but tragically, he will not be the last. His death should be held up as an example of why racial profiling is discriminatory and is a poor law enforcement technique. Furthermore, racial profiling makes the public distrust police officers and other law enforcement agents, making their jobs even more difficult. Hunting terrorists or other criminals based on their physical appearance puts millions of innocent people at risk while threatening the values we cherish. For all of these reasons, we must reject racial profiling.

How does the conclusion return to ideas discussed in the beginning of the essay?

Works Cited

Green, Mark. "Profiling Means Surrender in the War on Terrorism." HuffingtonPost.com 13 Aug 2005 < http://www.huffingtonpost.com/mark-green/profiling-means-surrender-b-5597.html > .

Exercise 2A: Identifying and Organizing Components of the Narrative Essay

As you read in Preface B of this section, narrative essays contain certain elements, including *characters*, *setting*, and *plot*. This exercise will help you identify these elements and place them in an organized structure of paragraphs.

For this exercise you will isolate and identify the components of a narrative essay. Model Essay Three, "Hatred at the Grocery Store," is a good source to practice on. You may also, if you choose, use experiences from your own life or that of your friends and family. Part of the exercise is filled out for you using the narrative elements from "Why Racial Profiling Does Not Work."

Part A: Isolate and write down story elements

Setting

The setting of a story is the time and place the story happens. Such information helps orient the reader. Does the story take place in the distant or recent past? Does it take place in a typical American community or exotic locale?

Model Essay Two	"Hatred at the Grocery Store"	Other Story
London Tube Station July 22, 2005		

Characters

Who is the story about? If there is more than one character, how are they related? At what stage of life are they? What are their aspirations and hopes? What makes them distinctive and interesting to the reader?

Model Essay Two	"Hatred at the Grocery Store"	Other Story
Jean Charles de Menezes 27-year-old electrician from Brazil		

Pivotal Event

Most stories contain at least one single, discrete event on which the narrative hinges. It can be a turning point that changes lives or a specific time when a character confronts a challenge, comes to a flash of understanding, or resolves a conflict.

Model Essay Two	"Hatred at the Grocery Store"	Other Story
Menezes is racially profiled as a terrorist suspect.		

Events/Actions Leading Up to the Pivotal Event

What are the events that happen to the characters? What are the actions the characters take? These elements are usually told in chronological order in a way that advances the action—that is, each event proceeds naturally and logically from the preceding one.

Model Essay Two	"Hatred at the Grocery Store"	Other Story
Terrorist attacks on London's subway system, the Tube, in preceding weeks have police on the lookout for terrorists of Arab or Southeast Asian descent who are acting suspiciously in or near the Tube.		

Events/Actions That Stem from Pivotal Event

What events/actions are the results of the pivotal event in the story? How were the lives of the characters of the stories changed?

Model Essay Two	"Hatred at the Grocery Store"	Other Story
Menezes is shot and killed; police later learn he is innocent.		

Point/Moral

What is the reason for telling the story? Stories generally have a lesson or purpose that is ultimately clear to the reader, whether the point is made explicitly or implied. Stories could serve as specific examples of a general social problem. They could be teaching tools describing behavior and actions that the reader should either avoid or emulate.

Model Essay Two	"Hatred at the Grocery Store"	Other Story
Story is an example of how racial profiling is a bad police technique that puts ordinary citizens in danger.		

Part B: Writing down narrative elements in paragraph form

Because stories vary greatly, there are many ways to approach telling them. One possible way of organizing the story elements you have structured is as follows:

Paragraph 1: Tell the reader the setting of the story and introduce the characters. Provide descriptive details of both.

Paragraph 2: Introduce the plot—what happens in the story. Tell the events in chronological order, with each event advancing the action.

Paragraph 3: Describe the pivotal event in detail and its immediate aftermath.

Paragraph 4: Tell the short-term and/or long-term ramifications of the pivotal event. This paragraph could also include the point or moral of the story.

Paragraph 5: Conclude the story in a memorable and interesting way.

Exercise 2B: Examining Introductions and Conclusions

Most essays feature introductory and concluding paragraphs that are used to frame the main ideas being presented. Along with presenting the essay's thesis statement, well-written introductions should grab the attention of the reader and make clear why the topic being explored is important. The conclusion reiterates the essay's thesis and is also the last chance for the writer to make an impression on the reader. Strong introductions and conclusions can greatly enhance an essay's effect on an audience.

The Introduction

There are several techniques that can be used to craft an introductory paragraph. An essay can start with:

- an anecdote: a brief story that illustrates a point relevant to the topic;
- startling information: facts or statistics that elucidate the point of the essay;
- setting up and knocking down a position: a position or claim believed by proponents of one side of a controversy, followed by statements that challenge that claim;

- historical perspective: an example of the way things used to be that leads into a discussion of how or why things work differently now;
- summary information: general introductory information about the topic that feeds into the essay's thesis statement.

Problem One

Reread the introductory paragraphs of the model essays and of the viewpoints in Section One. Identify which of the techniques described above are used in the example essays. How do they grab the attention of the reader? Are their thesis statements clearly presented?

The Conclusion

The conclusion brings the essay to a close by summarizing or returning to its main ideas. Good conclusions, however, go beyond simply repeating these ideas. Strong conclusions explore a topic's broader implications and reiterate why it is important to consider. They may frame the essay by returning to an anecdote featured in the opening paragraph. Or they may close with a quotation or refer to an event in the essay. In opinionated essays, the conclusion can reiterate which side the essay is taking or ask the reader to reconsider a previously held position on the subject.

Problem Two

Reread the concluding paragraphs of the model essays and of the viewpoints in Section One. Which were most effective in driving home their arguments to the reader? What sorts of techniques did they use to do this? Did they appeal emotionally to the reader or bookend an idea or event referenced elsewhere in the essay?

Hatred at the Grocery Store

Editor's Notes Essays drawn from memories or personal experiences are called personal narratives. The following essay is this type of narrative. It is not based on research or the retelling of someone else's experiences, as are the other narrative essays you have read in this book. Instead, this essay consists of an autobiographical story that recounts memories of an event that happened to the writer.

The essay differs from the first two model essays in that it is written from the subjective, or first-person ("I"), point of view. This type of narrative is called a personal narrative. It is important that you learn to master the personal narrative, as it is this type of essay that is frequently required by college, university, and other academic admissions boards. Personal narratives also tend to be required of candidates seeking to win scholarships and other contests.

The essay is also different from the previous model essays in that it has more than five paragraphs. Many ideas require more than five paragraphs in order to be adequately developed. Moreover, the ability to write a sustained essay is a valuable skill. Learning how to develop a longer piece of writing gives you the tools you will need to advance academically.

■ Refers to thesis and topic sentences

■ Refers to supporting details

Paragraph 1

The world is filled with more hate than I ever cared to imagine. I learned this lesson in a supermarket, of all places. I was picking up some groceries in the Orange Tree Market, a local grocery in my small, friendly California beach town. I watched my ricotta cheese, marinara sauce, and baguette float down the conveyor belt, thinking about the lasagna I would make for dinner that evening.

Because this is a personal narrative, it does not have the type of thesis statement a more formal essay should have. However, the main idea of the essay is still alluded to up front.

The cashier, a white woman in her forties covered in tattoos, seemed cheerful enough. As she scanned my items, she chatted away about the weather, her cat, a bar she had been to the night before.

Paragraph 3

"You just wouldn't be*lieve* the amount they charge just to get into these places nowadays. And for local bands, too! I remember paying a buck or two to get into some of these shows just a couple years ago."

I smiled and nodded. The price of everything was going up, it seemed.

"I mean, I wouldn't care if I made more money," she said.

"I hear you there," I said absentmindedly.

"The trouble is my Jew bosses—like every other Jew, they're stingy with their money and they don't pay us good."

I raised my head. What did she just say?

She continued. "I even gotta check my paycheck carefully to make sure they're not Jewing me out of my money, you know what I mean?"

Paragraph 4

The world slowed to down to a syrupy slow crawl. I could not believe she said what I had just heard her say. Panicked thoughts crowded my mind. Was she kidding? Did she know I was Jewish? What should I say? Did the people in line behind me hear her? I turned around— their saucer-sized eyes indicated they had. Furthermore, I happen to know the manager of the store is Italian, not Jewish, which seemed like a useless thing to point out to someone who was obviously bigoted and crazy.

Paragraph 5

I had no idea what to do or say. I felt frozen. "Um, you know, that's really not an appropriate comment to make." That was the best I could come up with.

Does the dialogue sound natural to you? What details or features enhance it?

"Oh come on. . . . You know they're like that—they're *all* like that." Suddenly, her smile turned into a sneer, and she squinted critically at me. "Wait a minute. . . . Ohhhh, I see what's going on here. You're a *Jew*, aren't you. You're one of 'em. Ha! Ok, ok. I get it. Ha!" She laughed to herself and continued to scan my items as if nothing had happened.

Paragraph 6

I turned around to gauge the other customers' reaction. Though they had all heard what the checker said, they pretended to be invisible. Some stared at the magazine rack; others focused their gaze on the tile floor. In addition to being taken off guard by the checker, I was astonished that no one—not a single person in line—was going to join me in countering this woman's prejudice.

Make a list of the specific details that have been used to bring the story to life. Such details include colors, objects, shapes, sizes, adjectives, and items. In *what instances* are these details used, and what do they add to the essay?

Paragraph 7

"Yes, I'm *Jewish*." I knew correcting her might just make her more hostile, but at this point, I figured I had nothing to lose. "And *you* are a bigot." I walked out of the store, leaving my groceries in an abandoned pile on the counter.

What have you learned about the characters up to this point? What details do you know of their lives? Are the characters being developed in a way that makes you care about them?

Paragraph 8

When I went home, I debated calling the store manager to report the woman's behavior. But I was not sure if that was the right thing to do—you usually do not change someone's mind by getting them in trouble. And yet it felt wrong to do nothing. After dinner that night, I considered my options while taking my dog Java on her evening walk.

Paragraph 9

As I circled the blocks, I thought about how to handle the situation. Lost in thought, I barely noticed that a white SUV was driving down the block straight toward me, showing no signs of slowing down.

How does this paragraph serve to move the plot forward?

Paragraph 10

The car screeched to a stop in front of me, and I jumped back, yanking Java's leash so hard she jumped. The driver's side window rolled down—it was the checker from the grocery store!

Paragraph 11

"Well hey there, *Jew!*" she screamed from the driver's seat. "My boss saw you leave the store in a huff today and fired me for talkin' wrong to the customers. Are you happy now, *Jew*?! Happy now?!"

She circled around me with her giant car, wheels screeching. I felt like a trapped animal. *How did she find me? What is she going to do?* was all I could think.

Paragraph 12

"You Jews are all the same," she cackled, maniacally. "You think you're *soooo* superior. Why do you think the whole world hates you?!"

I tried to run away from her car, but everywhere I turned, she cut me off. I was so scared Java was going to get trapped under those giant wheels.

"If I *ever* see you again, Jew, you're going to be sorry." Then she shouted some obscenities at me and screeched off, driving 50 mph down the dark, quiet street.

Paragraph 13

Can you picture the scene the author describes? What details allow you to visualize it best?

The whole incident could not have lasted more than ninety seconds, but I felt like my whole reality had been altered. I realized I was trembling, so I sat on the curb. Java looked at me as if to say, *What just happened?* "I have no idea, Java, I have no idea."

Paragraph 14

Thankfully, I never saw the woman again. But each of those terrifying ninety seconds became burned in my brain, a reminder of how cruel and hate-filled people can be. I used her hatred as a reminder that the world is an imperfect place, fraught with discrimination, racism, and misunderstanding. But rather than succumbing to that reality, I made it my mission to be the kind of person who acts as a force of good in the world, someone who counteracts the bigotry that exists in quiet corners and subtle moments. Most of all, I did not let the experience change me into a hateful person who is scared, ignorant, and bitter—the driving forces of bigotry and discrimination.

But I cannot say I ever shopped at the Orange Tree Market again.

Personal narratives are not expected to have a formal conclusion like other essays, but they must still bring the story's ideas to a close.

Exercise 3A: Practice Writing a Scene with Dialogue

The previous model essay used scene and dialogue to make a point. For this exercise, you will practice creative writing techniques to draft a one- or two-paragraph scene with dialogue. First, take another look at Model Essay Three, and examine how dialogue is used.

When writing dialogue, it is important to:

1. Use natural-sounding language.
2. Include a few details showing character gestures and expressions as they speak.
3. Avoid overuse of speaker tags with modifiers, such as "he said stupidly," "she muttered softly," "I shouted angrily," and so on.
4. Indent and create a new paragraph when speakers change.
5. Place quotation marks at the beginning and end of a character's speech. Do not enclose each sentence of a speech in quotation marks.

Scene-Writing Practice

Interview a classmate, friend, or family member. Focus on a specific question about discrimination, such as:

- Have you ever known anyone who has discriminated against someone else, or been discriminated against? If so, what was the situation? Who was involved? Where did it take place? What did they do about it?
- What would you do if you ever witnessed an act of discrimination? How would you feel? What might you say?
- Why do you think people discriminate against others?
- Did you live in a time period when discrimination was more commonplace? What was that era like?

Take notes while you interview your subject. Write down what he or she says, as well as any details that are provided. Ask probing questions that reveal how the subject felt, what they said, and how they acted. Be sure to establish a location for your scene, and include realistic descriptions of the place where the action occurred. Finally, use your notes and ideas to create a brief scene with dialogue.

But I Can't Write That

One aspect of personal narrative writing is that you are revealing to the reader something about yourself. Many people enjoy this part of writing, but others have trouble sharing their personal stories—especially if they reveal something embarrassing or something that could be used to get them in trouble. In these cases, what are your options?

✔ Talk with your teacher about your concerns. Will this narrative be shared in class? Can the teacher pledge confidentiality?

✔ Change the story from being about yourself to a story about a friend. This will involve writing in the third person rather than the first person.

✔ Change a few identifying details and names to disguise characters and settings.

✔ Pick a different topic or thesis that you do not mind sharing.

Exercise: Write Your Own Narrative Five-Paragraph Essay

Using the information from this book, write your own five-paragraph narrative essay that deals with discrimination. You can use the resources in this book for information about discrimination and how to structure a narrative essay.

The following steps are suggestions on how to get started.

Step One: Choose your topic.

The first step is to decide on what topic to write your narrative essay. Is there any subject that particularly fascinates you? Is there an issue you strongly support or feel strongly against? Is there a topic you feel personally connected to or have personal experience dealing with? Ask yourself such questions before selecting your essay topic. Refer to Appendix D: Sample Essay Topics if you need help selecting a topic.

Step Two: Write down questions and answers about the topic.

Before you begin writing, you will need to think carefully about what ideas your essay will contain. This is a process known as *brainstorming*. Brainstorming involves asking yourself questions and coming up with ideas to discuss in your essay. Possible questions that will help you with the brainstorming process include:

- Why is this topic important?
- Why should people be interested in this topic?
- How can I make this essay interesting to the reader?
- What question am I going to address in this paragraph or essay?
- What facts, ideas, or quotes can I use to support the answer to my question?

Questions especially for narrative essays include:

- Have I chosen a compelling story to examine?
- Does the story support my thesis statement?

- What qualities do my characters have? Are they interesting?
- Does my narrative essay have a clear beginning, middle, and end?
- Does my essay evoke a particular emotion or response from the reader?

Step Three: Gather facts, ideas, and anecdotes related to your topic.

This book contains several places to find information, including the viewpoints and the appendices. In addition, you may want to research the books, articles, and Web sites listed in Section Three or do additional research in your local library. You can also conduct interviews if you know someone who has a compelling story that would fit well in your essay.

Step Four: Develop a workable thesis statement.

Use what you have written down in steps two and three to help you articulate the main point or argument you want to make in your essay. It should be expressed in a clear sentence and make an arguable or supportable point.

Example:

Efforts to adopt a constitutional amendment banning gay marriage should be rejected—prohibiting people from marrying based on their sexual orientation is a violation of their civil rights and discriminatory.

> This could be the thesis statement of a narrative essay that uses stories about committed homosexual couples to argue that banning gay marriage discriminates against them.

Step Five: Write an outline or diagram.
1. Write the thesis statement at the top of the outline.
2. Write roman numerals I, II, and III on the left side of the page with A, B, and C under each numeral.
3. Next to each roman numeral, write down the best ideas you came up with in step three. These should all directly relate to and support the thesis statement.

4. Next to each letter write down information that supports that particular idea.

Step Six: Write the three supporting paragraphs.
Use your outline to write the three supporting paragraphs. Write down the main idea of each paragraph in sentence form. Do the same thing for the supporting points of information. Each sentence should support the paragraph of the topic. Be sure you have relevant and interesting details, facts, and quotes. Use transitions when you move from idea to idea to keep the text fluid and smooth. Sometimes, although not always, paragraphs can include a concluding or summary sentence that restates the paragraph's argument.

Step Seven: Write the introduction and conclusion.
See Exercise 2B for information on writing introductions and conclusions.

Step Eight: Read and rewrite.
As you read, check your essay for the following:
- ✔ Does the essay maintain a consistent tone?
- ✔ Do all paragraphs reinforce your general thesis?
- ✔ Do all paragraphs flow from one to the other? Do you need to add transition words or phrases?
- ✔ Have you quoted from reliable, authoritative, and interesting sources?
- ✔ Is there a sense of progression throughout the essay?
- ✔ Does the essay get bogged down in too much detail or irrelevant material?
- ✔ Does your introduction grab the reader's attention?
- ✔ Does your conclusion reflect on any previously discussed material or give the essay a sense of closure?
- ✔ Are there any spelling or grammatical errors?

**Section Three:
Supporting
Research
Material**

Facts About Discrimination

Editor's Note: These facts can be used in reports to reinforce or add credibility when making important points or claims.

Arab and Muslim Americans

According to a 2006 *USA Today*/Gallup poll:

- 39 percent of Americans said they felt at least some prejudice against Muslims.
- 39 percent of Americans said they favored requiring Muslims, including those who are U.S. citizens, to carry a special ID to help prevent future terrorist attacks.
- 22 percent of respondents said they would not want Muslims as neighbors.

A 2006 Quinnipiac University Polling Institute poll found:

- 60 percent of poll respondents said authorities should single out, or racially profile, people who look "Middle Eastern" for security screening at locations such as airports and train stations.
- 37 percent of poll respondents said authorities should not racially profile people who look "Middle Eastern."
- 3 percent were unsure.

According to a the Pew Research Center:

- 53 percent of Muslims living in America say it has become more difficult to be a Muslim in the United States since September 11 because of harassment, suspicion, and fear of Muslims.
- 51 percent of Muslim Americans are "very worried" or "somewhat worried" that Muslim women who wear a veil are treated poorly by other Americans.

According to a poll conducted by New America Media and Amnesty International USA:

- Arab Americans are more than three times more likely than non-Latino white people to have experienced racial profiling since the 9/11 attacks.
- About one-fifth of Arab Americans (21 percent) say they have experienced discrimination in their schools, workplace, or neighborhoods in the last three years.
- About one-tenth of Arab Americans (11 percent) said they have been victims of mistreatment or targeting by government officials because of race, ethnicity, religion, or national origin since 9/11; 87 percent said they had not.
- Nearly one-third of Pakistani Americans (31 percent) said they had experienced discrimination since 9/11.
- 15 percent of Muslims said they had experienced racial profiling in the last three years; 6 percent of non-Muslims said they had.
- 18 percent of Muslims report knowing someone who has been unfairly deported.

The Wage Gap

According to the U.S. Bureau of Labor Statistics, the median income for all women is about three-quarters that of men.

According to the WAGE Project, which tracks the differences in pay between men and women:

- The wage gap costs women between $700,000 and $2 million over the course of their careers.
- American women earn 76 cents for every dollar men earn.
- African American women earn 68 cents for every dollar men earn.
- Latinas earn 57 cents for every dollar men earn.
- Asian American and Pacific Islander American women earn 88 cents for every dollar men earn.

According to the National Center for Policy Analysis:

- Although women hold 53 percent of all professional jobs in the United States, they hold only 28 percent of jobs that pay more than $40,000 a year.
- Working mothers are nearly twice as likely to take time off to care for their children as are working fathers in two-income families.
- When women behave in the workplace as men do, the wage gap between them is small. Among 27- to 33-year-olds who have never had a child, women earn 98 percent of what men do.
- 71 percent of women prefer jobs with more flexibility and benefits than jobs with higher wages, and nearly 85 percent of women take these arrangements when they are available.

Affirmative Action

Just a few countries practice affirmative action policies. These include:

- China
- India
- Malaysia
- South Africa
- United States

According to the Coalition to Defend Affirmative Action, Integration & Immigrant Rights and Fight for Equality by Any Means Necessary (BAMN):

- When the ban on affirmative action was implemented at the University of California (UC)–Berkeley law school, the number of black students admitted dropped from 75 in 1996 to 14 (out of 792 applicants) in 1997; none enrolled.
- In its first year without affirmative action, the UC–San Diego School of Medicine did not admit a single black applicant of the 196 who applied.
- UC–Berkeley admitted 61 percent fewer minorities in 1998—the year the state first implemented its ban on affirmative action at the undergraduate level.

- Between 1890 and 1970 the percentage of lawyers who were black increased less than 1 percentage point: from 0.48 percent to 1.29 percent. Fifteen years later as a result of affirmative action policies, 5.1 percent of law students were black. In 1995, the last year affirmative action programs existed at every law school, black students composed 7.5 percent of all law students.

Finding and Using Sources of Information

No matter what type of essay you are writing, it is necessary to find information to support your point of view. You can use sources such as books, magazine articles, newspaper articles, and online articles.

Using Books and Articles

You can find books and articles in a library by using the library's computer or cataloging system. If you are not sure how to use these resources, ask a librarian to help you. You can also use a computer to find many magazine articles and other articles written specifically for the Internet.

You are likely to find a lot more information than you can possibly use in your essay, so your first task is to narrow it down to what is likely to be most usable. Look at book and article titles. Look at book chapter titles, and examine the book's index to see if it contains information on the specific topic you want to write about. (For example, if you want to write about racial profiling and you find a book about Muslim Americans, check the chapter titles and index to be sure it contains information related to racial profiling and discrimination specifically before you bother to check out the book.)

For a five-paragraph essay, you do not need a great deal of supporting information, so quickly try to narrow down your materials to a few good books and magazine or Internet articles. You do not need dozens. You might even find that one or two good books or articles contain all the information you need.

You probably do not have time to read an entire book, so find the chapters or sections that relate to your topic, and skim these. When you find useful information, copy it onto a note card or notebook. You should look for supporting facts, statistics, quotations, and examples.

Using the Internet

When you select your supporting information, it is important that you evaluate its source. This is especially important with information you find on the Internet. Because nearly anyone can put information on the Internet, there is as much bad information as good information. Before using Internet information—or any information—determine if the source seems to be reliable. Is the author or Internet site sponsored by a legitimate organization? Is it from a government source? Does the author have any special knowledge or training relating to the topic you are looking up? Does the article give any indication of where its information comes from?

Using Your Supporting Information

When you use supporting information from a book, article, interview, or other source, there are three important things to remember:

1. *Make it clear whether you are using a direct quotation or a paraphrase.* If you copy information directly from your source, you are quoting it. You must put quotation marks around the information and tell where the information comes from. If you put the information in your own words, you are paraphrasing it.

Here is an example of a using a quotation:

Journalist Salim Muwakkil explains that ethnic team names such as the Redskins or the Indians are a problem because they make light of decades, even centuries, of oppression and discrimination. "The fight against Native American mascots and logos," he says, "is a serious struggle to overturn the stereotypes and cultural assumptions that were forged in our racist past but still help determine the trajectory of our lives today."

Here is an example of a brief paraphrase of the same passage:

Journalist Salim Muwakkil explains that ethnic team names such as the Redskins or the Indians are a problem because they make light of decades, even centuries, of oppression and discrimination. They hurt because they make fun of horrible historical events that continue to inform peoples' lives even today. Attempts to prohibit them, therefore, should be viewed as serious antidiscrimination efforts.

2. *Use the information fairly.* Be careful to use supporting information in the way the author intended it. For example, it is unfair to quote an author as saying, "Affirmative action programs help," when he or she intended to say, "Affirmative action programs help lawmakers feel like they are doing something to address discrimination, but usually fail to address the underlying problem of discrimination in our society." This is called taking information out of context. This is using supporting evidence unfairly.

3. *Give credit where credit is due.* Giving credit is known as citing. You must use citations when you use someone else's information, but not every piece of supporting information needs a citation.

   • If the supporting information is general knowledge—that is, it can be found in many sources—you do not have to cite your source.
   • If you directly quote a source, you must cite it.
   • If you paraphrase information from a specific source, you must cite it.

If you do not use citations where you should, you are *plagiarizing*—or stealing—someone else's work.

Citing Your Sources

There are a number of ways to cite your sources. Your teacher will probably want you to do it in one of three ways:
   • Informal: As in the example in number I above, tell where you got the information as you present it in the text of your essay.

- Informal list: At the end of your essay, place an unnumbered list of all the sources you used. This tells the reader where, in general, your information came from.
- Formal: Use numbered footnotes or endnotes. Notes are generally placed at the end of an article or essay, although they may be placed elsewhere depending on your teacher's requirements.

Works Cited

Muwakkil, Salim. "Racial Slurs Taint U.S. Sports." Tolerance. org 14 Apr. 2006 < www.tolerance.org/news/article_tol. jsp?id = 1047 > .

Using MLA Style to Create a Works Cited List

You will probably need to create a list of works cited for your paper. These include materials that you quoted from, relied heavily on, or consulted to write your paper. There are several different ways to structure these references. The following examples are based on Modern Language Association (MLA) style, one of the major citation styles used by writers.

Book Entries

For most book entries you will need the author's name, the book's title, where it was published, what company published it, and the year it was published. This information is usually found on the inside of the book. Variations on book entries include the following:

A book by a single author:
> Friedman, Thomas. *Hot, Flat, and Crowded: Why We Need a Green Revolution—and How It Can Renew America*. New York: Farrar, Straus and Giroux, 2008.

Two or more books by the same author:
> Pollen, Michael. *Botany of Desire: A Plant's-Eye View of the World*. New York: Random House, 2002.
> ———. *The Omnivore's Dilemma: A Natural History of Four Meals*. New York: Penguin Books, 2006.

A book by two or more authors:
> Esposito, John L., and Dalia Mogahed. *Who Speaks for Islam? What a Billion Muslims Really Think*. Washington, DC: Gallup Press, 2008.

A book with an editor:
> Skancke, Jennifer S., ed. *Introducing Issues with Opposing Viewpoints: Stem Cell Research.* Detroit: Greenhaven, 2008.

Periodical and Newspaper Entries

Entries for sources found in periodicals and newspapers are cited a bit differently from books. For one, these sources usually have a title and a publication name. They also may have specific dates and page numbers. Unlike book entries, you do not need to list where newspapers or periodicals are published or what company publishes them.

An article from a periodical:
> Aldhous, Peter. "China's Burning Ambition." *Nature* 30 June 2005: 1152–55.

An unsigned article from a periodical:
> "Contraception in Middle School?" *Harvard Crimson* 21 Oct. 2007.

An article from a newspaper:
> Cunningham, Roseanna. "Care, Not Euthanasia, Is the Answer to the 'Problem' of the Elderly." *Sunday Times* [London] 20 Jul. 2008: 21.

Internet Sources

To document a source you found online, try to provide as much information on it as possible, including the author's name, the title of the document, date of publication or of last revision, the URL, and your date of access.

A Web source:
> Mieszkowski, Katharine. "Plastic Bags Are Killing Us." Salon.com. 10 Aug. 2007. 9 Sept. 2008 < http://www.salon.com/news/feature/2007/ 08/10/plastic_bags/index.html > .

Your teacher will tell you exactly how information should be cited in your essay. Generally, the very least information needed is the original author's name and the name of the article or other publication.

Be sure you know exactly what information your teacher requires before you start looking for your supporting information so that you know what information to include with your notes.

Sample Essay Topics

Discrimination Is a Serious Problem

Discrimination Is Not a Serious Problem

Discrimination Against African Americans Is Still a Problem

Discrimination Against African Americans Is No Longer a Problem

Discrimination Against Arab Americans Is on the Rise

Discrimination Against Arab Americans Is Not on the Rise

Discrimination Against Latinos Is Increasing

Latinos Are Rarely Discriminated Against

Women Are Discriminated Against in the Workplace

Women Are Rarely Discriminated Against in the Workplace

The Wage Gap Is a Result of Discrimination Against Women

The Wage Gap Is Not a Result of Discrimination Against Women

Racial Profiling Is Discriminatory

Racial Profiling Is Not Discriminatory

Racial Profiling Is Good Police Work

Racial Profiling Is Not Good Police Work

Ethnic Team Names Are Discriminatory

Ethnic Team Names Are Not Discriminatory

Banning Gay Marriage Is Discriminatory

Banning Gay Marriage Is Not Discriminatory

Race-Based Humor Is Discriminatory

Race-Based Humor Is Not Discriminatory

Affirmative Action Helps Overcome Discrimination

Affirmative Action Does Not Help Overcome Discrimination

Affirmative Action Discriminates Against White People

Writing Prompts for Personal Narratives

Use another person's story or your own story to illustrate any of the topics listed above, or come up with a unique topic on your own. Describe what happened during an incident when you, a person you know, or someone you read about was in a situation that involved discrimination. Use research, interviews, or personal experience to tell the story so that it supports the point you want to make about discrimination.

Organizations to Contact

The editors have compiled the following list of organizations concerned with the issues debated in this book. The descriptions are derived from materials provided by the organizations. All have publications or information available for interested readers. The list was compiled on the date of publication of the present volume; the information provided here may change. Be aware that many organizations take several weeks or longer to respond to queries, so allow as much time as possible.

American-Arab Anti-Discrimination Committee (ADC)
4201 Connecticut Ave. NW, Ste. 300, Washington, DC 20008
(202) 244-2990 • e-mail: adc@adc.org • Web site: www. adc.org

This organization fights anti-Arab stereotyping in the media and works to protect Arab Americans from discrimination and hate crimes. It publishes a bimonthly newsletter, the *Chronicle*; issue papers and special reports; community studies; legal, media, and educational guides; and action alerts.

American Association for Affirmative Action (AAAA)
888 Sixteenth St. NW, Ste. 800, Washington, DC 20006
(800) 252-8952 • Web site: www.affirmativeaction.org

The AAAA is a national nonprofit association of professionals who work in the areas of affirmative action, equal opportunity, and diversity. It strongly opposes federal or state action that would eliminate affirmative action programs that provide equal access and equity for minorities and women in employment, education, and economic opportunity.

American Civil Liberties Union (ACLU)

125 Broad St., 18th Flr., New York, NY 10004
(212) 549-2500 • fax: (212) 549-2646 • Web site: www.
aclu.org

The ACLU is a national organization that works to
defend Americans' civil rights as guaranteed by the U.S.
Constitution. The ACLU publishes and distributes policy
statements, pamphlets, and the semiannual newsletter
Civil Liberties Alert.

Cato Institute

1000 Massachusetts Ave. NW, Washington, DC 20001-
5403 • (202) 842-0200 • fax: (202) 842-3490
e-mail: cato@cato.org • Web site: www.cato.org

The Cato Institute is a libertarian public policy research
foundation dedicated to limiting the role of government
and protecting individual liberties. It researches claims of
discrimination and opposes affirmative action.

Center for Equal Opportunity

7700 Leesburg Pike, Ste. 231, Falls Church, VA 22043
(703) 442-0066 • Web site: www.ceousa.org

The Center for Equal Opportunity supports color-blind
public policies and seeks to block the expansion of racial
preferences and to prevent their use in employment, education, and voting. It publishes numerous documents on
affirmative action, immigration, voting, and other issues.

Center for the Study of Popular Culture (CSPC)

9911 W. Pico Blvd., Ste. 1290, Los Angeles, CA 90035
(310) 843-3699 • fax: (310) 843-3692 • Web site: www.
cspc.org

CSPC is a conservative educational organization that
addresses topics such as political correctness, cultural
diversity, and discrimination. Its civil rights project promotes equal opportunity for all individuals and provides
legal assistance to citizens challenging affirmative action.

Citizen's Commission on Civil Rights (CCCR)

2000 M St. NW, Ste. 400, Washington, DC 20036 • (202) 659-5565 • fax: (202) 223-5302 • e-mail: citizens@cccr.org
Web site: www.cccr.org

CCCR monitors the federal government's enforcement of antidiscrimination laws and promotes equal opportunity for all. It publishes reports on affirmative action and desegregation as well as the book *One Nation Indivisible: The Civil Rights Challenge for the 1990s.*

Commission for Racial Justice (CRJ)

700 Prospect Ave., Cleveland, OH 44115-1110
(216) 736-2100 • fax: (216) 736-2171

CRJ was formed in 1963 by the United Church of Christ in response to racial tensions gripping the nation at that time. Its goal is a peaceful, dignified society where all men and women are equal. CRJ publishes various documents and books, such as *Racism and the Pursuit of Racial Justice* and *A National Symposium on Race and Housing in the United States: Challenges for the 21st Century.*

Council on American-Islamic Relations (CAIR)

453 New Jersey Ave. SE, Washington, DC 20003
(202) 488-8787 • fax: (202) 488-0833 • e-mail: cair@cair-net.org • Web site: www.cair-net.org

CAIR is a nonprofit membership organization that presents an Islamic perspective to public policy issues and challenges the misrepresentation of Islam and Muslims. It fights discrimination against Muslims in America and lobbies political leaders on issues related to Islam. Its publications include the quarterly newsletter *CAIR News*, reports on Muslim civil rights issues, and periodic action alerts.

Equal Rights Marriage Fund (ERMF)

2001 M St. NW • Washington, DC 20036 • (202) 822-6546
fax: (202) 466-3540

The ERMF is dedicated to the legalization of gay and lesbian marriage and serves as a national clearinghouse for information on same-sex marriage. The organization publishes several brochures and articles, including *Gay Marriage: A Civil Right*.

The Heritage Foundation
214 Massachusetts Ave. NE, Washington, DC 20002-4999 (202) 546-4400 • fax: (202) 546-8328 • e-mail: info@heritage.org • Web site: www.heritage.org

The foundation is a conservative public policy research institute that advocates free-market principles, individual liberty, and limited government. It believes the private sector, not government, should be relied upon to ease social problems and to improve the status of minorities.

Hispanic Policy Development Project (HPDP)
1001 Connecticut Ave. NW, Ste. 901, Washington, DC 20036 • (202) 822-8414 • fax: (202) 822-9120

HPDP encourages the analysis of public policies affecting Hispanics in the United States, particularly the education, training, and employment of Hispanic youth. It publishes a number of books and pamphlets, including *Together Is Better: Building Strong Partnerships Between Schools and Hispanic Parents*.

National Association for the Advancement of Colored People (NAACP)
4805 Mt. Hope Dr., Baltimore, MD 21215-3297 • (410) 358-8900 • fax: (410) 486-9257

The NAACP is the oldest and largest civil rights organization in the United States. Its principal objective is to ensure the political, educational, social, and economic equality of minorities. It publishes the magazine *The Crisis* ten times a year as well as a variety of newsletters, books, and pamphlets.

National Committee on Pay Equity (NCPE)

555 New Jersey Ave. NW, Washington, DC 20001-2029
(703) 920-2010 • fax: (703) 979-6372 • e-mail: fairpay@
pay-equity.org • Web site: www.pay-equity.org

NCPE is a national coalition of labor, women's, and civil rights organizations and individuals working to achieve pay equity by eliminating sex- and race-based wage discrimination. Its publications include a quarterly newsletter, *Newsnotes*, and numerous books and briefing papers on the issue of pay equity.

National Network for Immigrant and Refugee Rights (NNIRR)

310 Eighth St., Ste. 303, Oakland, CA 94607 • (510) 465-1984
fax: (510) 465-1885 • e-mail: nnirr@igc.apc.org
Web site: www.nnirr.org

The network includes community, church, labor, and legal groups committed to the cause of equal rights for all immigrants. These groups work to end discrimination and unfair treatment of illegal immigrants and refugees. It publishes a monthly newsletter, *Network News*.

National Urban League

120 Wall St., 8th Flr., New York, NY 10005 • (212) 558-5300
fax: (212) 344-5332 • Web site: www.nul.org

A community service agency, the National Urban League aims to eliminate institutional racism in the United States. It also provides services for minorities who experience discrimination in employment, housing, welfare, and other areas. It publishes the report *The Price: A Study of the Costs of Racism in America* and the annual *State of Black America*.

The Prejudice Institute

Stephens Hall Annex, Towson State University, Towson, MD 21204-7097 • (410) 830-2435 • fax: (410) 830-2455

The Prejudice Institute is a national research center concerned with violence and intimidation motivated by prejudice. It conducts research, supplies information on model programs and legislation, and provides education and training to combat prejudicial violence. The Prejudice Institute publishes research reports, bibliographies, and the quarterly newsletter *Forum*.

United States Commission on Civil Rights

624 Ninth St. NW, Ste. 500, Washington, DC 20425
(202) 376-7533 • publications: (202) 376-8128

A fact-finding body, the commission reports directly to Congress and the president on the effectiveness of equal opportunity laws and programs. A catalog of its numerous publications can be obtained from its Publication Management Division.

Bibliography

Books

Aguirre, Adalberto, and Jonathan H. Turner, *American Ethnicity: The Dynamics and Consequences of Discrimination.* New York: McGraw-Hill, 2008.

Babcock, Linda, and Sara Laschever, *Women Don't Ask: Negotiation and the Gender Divide.* New Jersey: Princeton University Press, 2003.

Farrell, Warren, *Why Men Earn More: The Startling Truth Behind the Pay Gap—and What Women Can Do About It.* New York: AMACOM/American Management Association, 2004.

Friedman, Joel William, *Employment Discrimination Stories.* Westbury, NY: Foundation Press, 2006.

Kellough, J. Edward, *Understanding Affirmative Action: Politics, Discrimination, and the Search for Justice.* Washington, DC: Georgetown University Press, 2006.

Lang, Kevin, *Poverty and Discrimination.* Princeton NJ: Princeton University Press, 2007.

Schiller, Bradley R., *The Economics of Poverty and Discrimination.* Englewood Cliffs, NJ: Prentice Hall, 2007.

Lu-In Wang, *Discrimination by Default: How Racism Becomes Routine.* New York: New York University Press, 2006.

Periodicals

Chapman, Steve, "The Racial Profiling Myth Lives On," *RealClearPolitics*, May 6, 2007. www.realclearpolitics.com/articles/2007/05/the_racial_profiling_myth_live.html.

Council on American-Islamic Relations, "The Status of Muslim Civil Rights in the United States 2007: Presumption of Guilt," 2007. www.cair.com/pdf/2007-Civil-Rights-Report.pdf.

Driver, Shanta, "Combating the New Jim Crow in California," *California Progress Report*, November 6, 2007. www.californiaprogressreport.com/2007/11/combating_the_n.html.

Economist, "The Forgotten Underclass; Poor Whites," October 28, 2006.

Fears, Darryl, "Hispanics Cite Rise in Discrimination: Immigration Debate Is Called a Factor," *Washington Post*, July 14, 2006. www.washingtonpost.com/wpdyn/content/article//2006/07/13/AR2006071301552.html.

Ferguson, Barbara, "Thinking of Flying? Be Prepared for Racial Profiling," *Arab News*, August 25, 2006. www.arabnews.com/?page = 4&section = 0&article = 78320 &d = 25&m = 8&ym = 2006.

Harcourt, Bernard E., "Muslim Profiles Post 9/11: Is Racial Profiling an Effective Counterterrorist Measure and Does It Violate the Right to Be Free from Discrimination?" Public Law and Legal Theory Working Paper no. 123, Law School, University of Chicago, April 2006. www.law.uchicago.edu/academics/publiclaw/123.pdf.

Kelly, Raina, "Let's Talk About Race; In the Aftermath of Michael Richards's Meltdown at the Laugh Factory, It's Time to Tell the Truth About What's Too Scary to Say Out Loud," *Newsweek*, December 4, 2006.

Liddle, Rod, "Black People Are Shooting Each Other Because We Treat Them as a 'Community,'" *Spectator*, February 24, 2007.

Navarrette, Ruben, "Racial Profiling Is Un-American," *RealClearPolitics*, August 16, 2006. www.realclearpolitics.com/articles/2006/08/racial_profiling_is_unamerican.html.

Salaita, Steven, "The New Civilian Terrorists: Anti-Arab Racism Shapes the U.S. Discussion of the Middle East," *Colorlines Magazine*, January/February 2007.

Soto, José J., "When Will Affirmative Action, Equity, and Diversity Initiatives as Tools for Social Justice Become

Unnecessary, Unwarranted, and Anachronistic?"
InMotion, April 5, 2008. www.inmotionmagazine.com/
opin/jsoto_aa_08.html.

Williams, Walter, "Racial Profiling," *Jewish World Review*,
December 20, 2006. http://jewishworldreview.com/
cols/williams122006.php3.

Zetter, Kim, "Why Racial Profiling Doesn't Work," Salon.
com, August 22, 2005. http://dir.salon.com/story/
news/feature/2005/08/22/racial_profiling.

Web Sites

Adversity.net (www.adversity.net). This Web site, started in 1997 to promote fair and equal treatment under
the law without regard to race, gender, or ethnicity,
contains information on ways in which affirmative
action has hurt Americans.

American Muslim Council (http://www.amcnational.
org). Founded in 1990, this organization seeks to
increase the political participation of Muslim Americans.
The Web site has the group's history, current projects,
news releases, and links to more than three dozen other
Islamic Web sites.

Americans Against Discrimination and Preferences
(www.aadap.org). This Web site is authored by the
backers of California's Proposition 209, which prohib-
ited the use of preferences in that state's public university admission policies. It contains news articles, legal
briefs, and other informative updates.

Asian Nation (www.asian-nation.org). Covers issues of
importance to the Asian American community.

**BAMN—the Coalition to Defend Affirmative Action by
Any Means Necessary** (www.bamn.com/index.asp).
A pro–affirmative action site that contains numerous
links to news and feature stories about affirmative
action.

The Black Commentator (www.blackcommentator.com). A Web site published for an African American audience. Contains numerous cartoons, articles, essays, and links to other resources about contemporary issues facing African Americans.

Hate Crimes Research Network (www.hatecrime.net). Based at Portland State University in Oregon, the HCRN links work done by sociologists, criminologists, psychologists, and others on the topic of hate crimes. The goal is to create a common pool of research and data to understand the phenomenon of hate crime.

Hispanic Online (www.hispaniconline.com). A site containing a wealth of information related to the Hispanic community.

National Organization for Women (www.now.org). The National Organization for Women (NOW) is the largest organization of feminist activists in the United States. NOW works to eliminate discrimination and harassment in the workplace, schools, the justice system, and all other sectors of society; secure abortion, birth control and reproductive rights for all women; end all forms of violence against women; eradicate racism, sexism, and homophobia; and promote equality and justice in society.

Race, Gender, and Affirmative Action: A Resource Page for Teaching (www.personal.umich.edu/~eandersn/biblio.htm). Teachers designing courses on race, gender, and affirmative action may find this Web site, maintained by a professor at the University of Michigan, especially helpful.

Index

Picture Credits

About the Editor

Lauri S. Friedman earned her bachelor's degree in religion and political science from Vassar College in Poughkeepsie, New York. Her studies there focused on political Islam. Friedman has worked as a nonfiction writer, a newspaper journalist, and an editor for more than eight years. She has extensive experience in both academic and professional writing settings.

Lauri is the founder of LSF Editorial, a writing and editing business in San Diego. Her clients include Greenhaven Press, for whom she has edited and authored numerous publications on controversial social issues such as oil, the Internet, the Middle East, democracy, pandemics, and obesity. Every book in the *Writing the Critical Essay* series has been under her direction or editorship, and she has personally written more than eighteen titles in the series. She was instrumental in the creation of the series and played a critical role in its conception and development.